EatingWell™

serves two

Library of Congress Cataloging-in-Publication Data.

Eating well serves two : 150 healthy in a hurry suppers / Jim Romanoff and the test kitchens of
Eating well.

p. cm.

Includes index.

ISBN-13: 978-0-88150-723-2

ISBN-10: 0-88150-723-7

1. Cookery for two. 2. Quick and easy cookery. I. Romanoff, Jim. II. Eating well. III. Title:
Eating well serves.

TX652.E3188 2006

641.5'612–dc22

2006046317

Editor: Jim Romanoff

Contributing Writer & Editor: Marialisa Calta

Managing Editor: Wendy S. Ruopp   **Assistant Managing Editor:** Alesia Depot

Test Kitchen: Stacy Fraser (Test Kitchen Manager), Jessica Price (Associate Food Editor),
Carolyn Malcoun (Assistant Editor), Katie Webster (recipe developer, food stylist),
Carolyn Casner, Elizabeth Sengle, Patsy Jamieson (food stylist)

Associate Nutrition Editor: Sylvia Geiger, M.S., R.D.

Production Manager: Jennifer B. Brown

Research Editor: Anne C. Treadwell   **Proofreader:** David Grist

Art Director: Michael J. Balzano   **Photographer:** Ken Burris

Front cover photograph: Chicken Tacos with Charred Tomatoes (*page 128*)
Additional photographs: Jim Scherer (*page 35*), Steven Mark Needham/Envision (*page 45*)
Illustrations: Michael J. Balzano
Jacket Design: Vertigo Design NYC

Published by
The Countryman Press, P.O. Box 748, Woodstock, Vermont 05091

Distributed by
W.W. Norton & Company, Inc., 500 Fifth Avenue, New York, New York 10110

10 9 8 7 6 5 4

EatingWell™
serves two

150 healthy in a hurry suppers

JIM ROMANOFF
and the test kitchens of

The Countryman Press
Woodstock, Vermont

Acknowledgments

Although my name goes on the cover of *EatingWell Serves Two*, it has truly been a group endeavor. Special thanks to: Jessie Price and Carolyn Malcoun for their invaluable work in helping to compile and edit this volume; it would never have gotten done without them. Thanks to Carolyn Casner and Beth Sengle for their diligence in testing (and retesting) these recipes, and to Katie Webster for her innovative and creative work as a recipe developer and food stylist. Thanks to Stacy Fraser for keeping our test kitchen standards unsurpassable and making it run like a brand-new food processor. Thanks to art director Mike Balzano, who came late to this project but added excellent style and refinement to the book. To Ken Burris, whose beautiful photography always makes our food look enticing. To Marialisa Calta, for her eloquent polishing of words and constant good humor. Also I thank Wendy Ruopp for keeping this project on track and always making me think twice. Most important, thanks to my family for keeping me grounded and making all my efforts worthwhile.

—*J.R.*

Recipe Guidelines & Nutrient Analyses

Defining "Active minutes" and "Total":

Testers in the EATINGWELL Test Kitchen keep track of the time needed for each recipe. **Active Minutes** includes prep time (the time it takes to chop, dice, puree, mix, combine, etc. before cooking begins), but it also includes the time spent tending something on the stovetop, in the oven or on the grill—and getting it to the table. If you can't walk away from it, we consider it active minutes. **Total** includes both active and inactive minutes and indicates the entire amount of time required for each recipe, start to finish. **To Make Ahead** gives storage instructions to help you plan. If special **Equipment** is needed, we tell you that at the top of the recipe too.

Analysis Notes:

Each recipe is analyzed for calories, total fat, saturated (SAT) and monounsaturated (MONO) fat, cholesterol, carbohydrate, protein, fiber, sodium and potassium. (Numbers less than 0.5 are rounded down to 0; 0.5 to 0.9 are rounded up to 1.) We use Food Processor SQL software (ESHA Research) for analyses.

When a recipe states a measure of salt "or to taste," we analyze the measured quantity. (Readers on sodium-restricted diets can reduce or eliminate the salt.) Recipes are tested with iodized table salt unless otherwise indicated. Kosher or sea salt is called for when the recipe will benefit from the unique texture or flavor. We assume that rinsing reduces the sodium in canned beans by 35%.

Butter is analyzed as unsalted. We do not include trimmings or marinade that is not absorbed. When alternative ingredients are listed, we analyze the first one suggested. Optional ingredients and garnishes are not analyzed. Portion sizes are consistent with healthy-eating guidelines.

Nutrition Icons:

Our nutritionists have highlighted recipes likely to be of interest to those following various dietary plans. Recipes that meet specific guidelines are marked with these icons:

Healthy ⨞ Weight

An entree has reduced calories, carbohydrate, fats and saturated fats, as follows:

CALORIES ≤ 350, CARBS ≤ 33g, TOTAL FAT ≤ 20g, SAT FAT ≤ 10g

Lower ⬇ Carbs

Recipe has 22 grams or less of carbohydrate per serving.

High ⬆ Fiber

Recipe provides 5 grams or more of fiber per serving.

Nutrition Bonuses:

Nutrition bonuses are indicated for recipes that provide 15% or more of the daily value (dv) of specific nutrients. The daily values are the average daily recommended nutrient intakes for most adults that you see listed on food labels. In addition to the nutrients listed on food labels (vitamins A and C, calcium, iron and fiber), we have included bonus information for other nutrients, such as folate, magnesium, potassium, selenium and zinc, when a recipe is particularly high in one of these. We have chosen to highlight these nutrients because of their importance to good health and the fact that many Americans may have inadequate intakes of them.

CONTENTS

Healthy in a Hurry for Two

Perhaps you're a single who has become a twosome, a couple whose kids have grown and flown, roommates, life-mates... whatever. You're health-conscious and you love good food, but you don't have the time or desire to spend a major portion of every day shopping and cooking to get a good meal on the table. You want to avoid the nutritional and economic downsides of the supermarket's prepared entrees and take-out restaurant food—you want the satisfaction of a delicious and healthy home-cooked meal. Yet, you quickly learn, cooking out of traditional cookbooks and food magazines leaves you with an eternity of leftovers or struggling to "do the math" to pare down those recipes to two servings. *EatingWell Serves Two* is the solution.

At EATINGWELL Magazine, many of us are in the same boat you are and we're here to help. In setting out to make quick, tasty, healthy meals for two, our Test Kitchen team, half of whom cook for two at home, quickly discovered that merely scaling down our existing recipes just wasn't going to cut it for this book. That's why we started from scratch. The new recipes are based on the principles behind our popular *Healthy in a Hurry* column: recipes that are foolproof, with outstanding flavor, ingredients and visual appeal plus great nutrition credentials—recipes that can all be made in 45 minutes or less (under 30 minutes, in some cases). Plus we make sure to select ingredients available in most larger supermarkets so you can count on one-stop shopping for these meals. We've also included special sections to give you ideas for quick side dishes, sauces and dressings, a guide to different methods for cooking 20 vegetables and, to finish your meals, some tempting desserts.

In creating this book, we've faced the same cooking conundrums that you face, especially when it comes to package sizes. A "family size" pack of chicken parts or a 2-pound bag of spring greens wasn't going to work for two people sitting down to dinner on a Tuesday night. Sure, you can freeze the extra chicken, but what about those greens? We learned to seek out supermarkets with consumer-friendly meat counters that will package up a smaller amount, markets that sell produce loose or precut and washed but in smaller bags. And while it may seem expensive to buy the small can of chickpeas when that jumbo can is such a bargain, we quickly learned that, much as we may love chickpeas, a two-week diet of them quickly loses its appeal (*see "Just Enough for Two," page 11*).

We've learned a thing or two about kitchen equipment in putting this book together. A quick sauté of chicken breasts with a sauce made by deglazing the pan sounds tempting and delicious—and it is. But sauté that chicken in a 12-inch skillet and the liquid for the sauce will evaporate in a nanosecond, and the chicken itself may burn. The right-size pan—in this case, an 8- or 10-inch skillet—is essential when couples are cooking (*see "Tool Smarts," page 13*).

We know that you want to spend your food dollars wisely. To that end, we've scrutinized prepared convenience products and use them judiciously. Sure, frozen vegetables, prewashed salad mixes and canned broths do, without a doubt, shave prep time without sacrificing quality, but many convenience products are loaded with salt and hydrogenated fat, along with objectionable or downright unpleasant tastes. We're here to help you figure out which ones are worth buying.

We know that you crave variety. One of the reasons you're not making a chili that serves eight—and then eating it for four nights running—is that you want to enjoy the widest possible assortment of healthful foods available. Of course, when you find that recipe you can't live without, we won't complain if you double it and serve it again, or bring it to work tomorrow. We've learned that it's much easier to double a recipe than to halve it.

Finally, we think we have been exhaustive in anticipating your cooking-for-two needs. You want great flavors, healthy meals, quick and smart suggestions. With *EatingWell Serves Two*, you now have the recipes, the shopping tips and the specialized cooking secrets to prepare hundreds of different nutritious meals for yourself and your dinner companion.

—*Jim Romanoff*
EATINGWELL *Food Editor*
Charlotte, Vermont

The EatingWell Test Kitchen team at their local market: Jim Romanoff, Carolyn Casner, Jessie Price, Carolyn Malcoun, Katie Webster, Elizabeth Sengle, Stacy Fraser

Getting It Together

Let's face it—you're pressed for time. Commitments to work, family and community compete with your free time—your time to exercise, see family and friends, read a book or watch a movie—your time to relax. Dinner preparations easily become an afterthought. Picking up some take-out on your way home seems like the time-saving way to go, especially for a twosome. After all, you can each eat what you're in the mood for and if it's a little heavy on the fat and salt, a little light on the fiber and nutrients, and a little hard on the wallet, it's only one meal! But a healthy diet is built one meal at a time, and if you're craving delicious, healthy, homemade meals, this book will enable you to prepare them quickly and easily… just for the two of you.

Before you put the local pizza joint or noodle house on speed-dial or fill your freezer with frozen entrees, consider that many prepared foods are overloaded with calories and fat, as well as added sweeteners and sodium. Plus, they frequently deliver more of the cheap, less desirable carbohydrates (white flour, white rice, white sugar, white potatoes) than any of us really need. Home cooking can be our best strategy to avoid such nutritional pitfalls.

Consider that food we make ourselves provides the satisfying flavors and textures that take-out and processed foods usually fail to deliver. Preparing food for ourselves gives us the option of using the best, freshest, most delicious ingredients—and the security of knowing that we are doing the right thing for ourselves and our partners. And when we're cooking for two, we can even splurge a bit on foods that might be unaffordable for a crowd.

Cooking well for two does have its challenges, as anyone knows who has tried to break down that recipe that serves 4… or 6… or 8 and wound up trying to measure ⅙ teaspoon of an herb or to halve an egg. That's where the EATINGWELL Test Kitchen shines; our staff has created recipes for two, rather than starting with larger recipes and trying to pare them down. We've figured out what tools work best in the kitchen-for-two, and identified a few necessary skills that anyone can master.

But whether we are cooking for two or 20, some of the same truths apply: we need to be mindful of what we are doing, we need to shop with an eye toward taking time-saving, but nutritionally satisfying, shortcuts, we need an organized, properly equipped kitchen—and we need the right recipes.

The advice and recipes that follow are all you need to start cooking for two in your own kitchen.

Planning It Out

When you go on a car trip, you have an idea of where you're going, but a map is going to help you get there by the most direct route. A menu plan will help you get from grocery store to table with the least amount of stress.

1. Draw it up: Take a few minutes at the beginning of each week to plan your meals for the coming days. Check your and your partner's schedule for dinner conflicts like late nights at work or evening classes. Whatever you do, don't wait until you get home from work to figure out what's for dinner. That's just an invitation to order in pizza or Chinese.

2. Write it down: Make a detailed shopping list, grouping what you need based on the layout of your favorite market. It's a drag to find yourself buying yogurt in the dairy aisle only to realize you forgot the cilantro back in produce. A list saves time and it can save money; if you stick to it, you'll avoid those "impulse" buys.

3. Work ahead: Consider cooking two meals on a leisurely weekend or weeknight evening, and reheating on a busier day. Even fresh vegetables like green beans and broccoli can be made ahead; blanch them at the start of the week and store them in resealable bags. Quickly rewarmed or sautéed and then seasoned, these make for almost-instant side dishes.

4. Minimize waste. If a recipe calls for, say, half a bell pepper, you don't want to throw out the other half. Look to our "Quick Sides" (*page 227*) and "Tips for Two" (*page 247*) sections for ideas on how to use leftover products. We've also profiled our favorite ingredients for two and shopping-for-two tips in "Just Enough for Two" (*page 11*).

Shopping Savvy

Remember your mission: getting healthy, tasty meals for two on the table in a reasonable amount of time. These recipes will guide you to quick-cooking cuts of meat and poultry—chops, cutlets and fillets—which keep cooking time to a minimum.

Our recipes will also help you choose convenience products wisely, to save money and avoid waste. While broths and other prepared products, such as canned tomatoes and beans, are lifesavers at times, they can be loaded with salt and sometimes short on flavor. Experiment to find out which brands appeal to you the most and always read the labels to avoid ending up with a lot of unwanted ingredients.

You've got your shopping list, but you still need to keep your wits about you. Follow our top five tips (*page 10*) for gathering the raw materials for a meal.

THE WELL-STOCKED PANTRY

Oils, Vinegars & Condiments

- Extra-virgin olive oil for cooking and salad dressings

- Canola oil for cooking and baking

- Flavorful nut and seed oils for salad dressings and stir-fry seasonings: toasted sesame oil, walnut oil

- Butter, preferably unsalted. Store in the freezer if you use infrequently.

- Reduced-fat mayonnaise

- Vinegars: balsamic, red-wine, white-wine, rice, cider

- Asian condiments and flavorings: reduced-sodium soy sauce, fish sauce, hoisin sauce, mirin, oyster sauce, chile-garlic sauce, curry paste

- Kalamata olives, green olives

- Dijon mustard

- Capers

- Ketchup

- Barbecue sauce

- Worcestershire sauce

1. **Know your market.** Seek out and patronize the supermarket with a friendly meat and fish counter, where you can buy two chicken breasts or salmon fillets instead of prewrapped packages of "family size" chicken pieces or a shrink-wrapped side of salmon. Likewise, a supermarket offering loose produce will allow you to buy just that one zucchini you need for the recipe or just enough green beans for two—not bags of produce that will wilt or rot before you get a chance to use them. This means fresher foods, less waste and fewer leftovers.

2. **Be picky.** Ripe fruits and vegetables cook faster and add much more flavor than their immature counterparts. But how do you tell what's ripe? Some occasional squeezing is required (with an avocado there's no other way), but you usually don't have to manhandle the merchandise. There is, in fact, one cardinal rule for almost all fruits and vegetables: if it doesn't smell like anything, it won't taste like anything. Forgo the smell-less (and thus, tasteless) stuff and go for what's ripe, fresh and ready to cook.

The same goes for meat and fish. Ask the person behind the counter if you can smell before you buy. Fish and shellfish should smell like blue ocean at high tide on a spring morning, never like the tidal flats on an August afternoon. Meat should smell clean and bright, not like copper, soured yogurt or runny cheese.

The folks at the meat and fish counters may hide when they see you coming, but anyone sharing your table will be smitten by the full flavor and high quality of your food. After all, underripe or spoiled ingredients only mean a disappointing dinner—or even a delay while you head back to the supermarket or speed-dial for pizza.

3. **Think small.** Large packages may seem economical, but the small can will supply you with just enough for tonight's chili without any leftovers that may end up in the compost. Small cans of broth, small containers of yogurt, small packages of cheeses... these all have a place in the kitchen when you're cooking for two. And you may find the supermarket's salad bar to be your salvation: it's just the place to get a handful of diced onion or celery. The price per pound may be higher than if you bought the whole vegetable, but you'll have exactly what you need, with no waste.

4. **Buy time-saving, waste-minimizing precut or frozen fruits and vegetables.** Prewashed salad mixes might cost more than whole heads, but you often end up with less waste and more variety; and if you find a market that sells the greens from a bulk bin, you won't have any leftovers wilting in the vegetable drawer of the fridge. Likewise, if your choice is between a whole head of broccoli and bulk or frozen florets, you may want to choose the latter, and just use what you need when you need it. Of course, you wouldn't use frozen vegetables in a recipe that showcases fresh ones, but you can take them right

Just Enough for Two

In a world of warehouse clubs and big-box stores, it's increasingly hard for folks cooking for two to find items in the sizes they need. Here's a list of the shopping strategies and products we found that serve the cause.

IN THE PRODUCE SECTION

- Shop at a supermarket in your area with a produce department that offers loose fruits and vegetables rather than mega-portions wrapped in bulk packages. Larger items, like melons and cabbage, are often sold in halves or quarters as well.

- Packages of fresh mixed herbs, often labeled "poultry season-ing," "seafood blend" and "soup and stew blend," combine sprigs of several fresh herbs in one package. Check the label for which herbs are included in the package to see what fits your needs best for the upcoming week. (*See "Tips for Two," page 247, for storage tips and additional uses for leftover fresh herbs.*)

- Six-ounce bags of greens, such as spinach, arugula, watercress and mixed salad greens, are perfect for serving a pair.

- Consider tubes of pureed herbs, like Gourmet Gardens brand, which store well in your refrigerator or freezer. This way you won't end up wasting nearly an entire bunch of herbs if you only need a few sprigs.

- Small, individual vegetables, particularly onions, are often easier to find in the organic section.

- Fresh prepackaged mixed stir-fry vegetables are good for two.

- Large supermarkets often carry washed, precut fruits and vegetables so you can buy just the amount you need.

- Avoid waste, use the salad bar! A full container of cherry tomatoes or a whole bag of shredded cabbage may be an impractical purchase, so select just what you need at the salad bar.

IN THE MEAT & SEAFOOD DEPARTMENTS

- Identify markets with good butcher and/or seafood counters, where you can order exactly the amount of meat, chicken, fish or seafood you need. If your local supermarket only sells prepackaged meats that are more than you'll use right away, wrap the extras tightly and freeze them. A vacuum sealer is a great way to ensure the quality of frozen food.

- The 6- or 7-ounce cans and pouches of tuna, salmon, sardines and crab are perfect for two.

- If you need shrimp, buy peeled frozen tail-on shrimp. These are usually sold in 2-pound bags but you can take out what you need when you need it without having to defrost the whole amount. Some supermarkets also have bulk freezer bins of shrimp.
- A 2-pound bag of mussels yields about 6 ounces cooked meat, the appropriate portion for two diners.

IN THE AISLES
- One 14-ounce can of broth works well when making soups for two. When you only need part of a can of broth for a recipe, freeze the rest of the can to add to sauces and soups at a later date or try using a low-sodium bouillon, such as Herb-Ox. (*See "Tips for Two," page 247.*)

- The 7- and 8-ounce cans of beets, chickpeas and regular and no-salt-added tomato sauce are just the right size and handy to have on hand for dinner.
- Small drink boxes of 100% juice are convenient for making sauces and salad dressings, without a lot of extra juice left over.
- Dried herb blends, such as herbes de Provence and Italian seasoning, cut down on the number of spice jars in your cupboard.
- Utilize bulk bins, most often found in the natural-foods section of your supermarket or at natural-foods stores, to buy just the right amount of grains, nuts and dried fruits.
- Substitute whole-wheat pita breads for a large ball of dough when making pizza. It's quicker, and you won't be tempted to eat more than your share. Leftover pitas freeze well too.
- Fruits and vegetables individually quick-frozen (IQF) before being bagged allow you to take out exactly what you need to defrost, keeping the rest of the bag frozen.

IN THE DAIRY SECTION
- Butter stores safely in your freezer for up to 6 months.
- Many markets have precut cheeses in smaller portions in the specialty cheese section. Or try a specialty cheese shop if there's one in your area. Use a vacuum sealer to store larger portions of cheese.
- Buy smaller servings of dairy products—pints of milk, 6- and 8-ounce containers of yogurt, 4-ounce containers of cottage cheese and 3-ounce blocks of cream cheese.

from the freezer to your skillet for any cooked dish. At any rate, always look for good-quality vegetables in the freezer case or produce section, and don't buy those doped with salt solutions or chemical preservatives.

A note about convenience foods: New convenience items are appearing with great regularity these days. We like containers of peeled garlic cloves, refrigerated jars of chopped ginger, and those newly available tubes of pureed herbs. When shopping for two, a smart buy might be packages of mixed fresh herbs—sold variously as "poultry seasoning," "soup seasoning" or "Italian seasoning." Frozen and pan-ready mushrooms, onions, peppers and other ingredients can make speedy cooking a reality.

5. **Be pantry smart** (*see "The Well-Stocked Pantry," pages 10, 13-16*). A full cupboard helps you avoid the there's-nothing-to-eat-so-let's-go-out moment. Of course, you needn't run out and buy this list before you start; it's just a handy list of things that will keep for months on end. Always plan on restocking essential pantry items when they run low.

Tool Smarts

If you've got kitchen envy from watching those remodeling shows on television or looking at glossy magazine ads or your neighbors' redesign, take a deep breath and repeat to yourself: "It's all about getting dinner on the table." And that you can do, even if you don't have a professional range or built-in wok. Don't get us wrong: the kitchen should be a pleasant place to work, but in the end, you just need to make sure your pots and tools are handy, your sink is cleared out and work surfaces are clean.

And you need a few good tools. Those cooking primarily for two will want to keep their smallest pans at hand and store the larger ones away for the days when company's coming. Using large pots and skillets for small amounts of food means that liquids may evaporate too quickly (hey! where'd the sauce go?) and that foods will burn more easily.

Here's our list of must-haves:

1. **Measuring spoons and cups:** One full set of measuring spoons, two full sets of measuring cups. We like having one set of measuring containers—the kind that come complete with handles and pour spouts—for liquids, and one graduated set—the kind that can be used to scoop out an ingredient and can be leveled off—for dry ingredients. Remember that measuring is vital for taste and portion control, and can be critical when working with just enough food for two. Try playing fast and loose when you're measuring, say, cayenne pepper, and you'll become a quick convert to good measuring tools.

2. **Cutting boards:** Ideally, there should be one that you use for produce and

THE WELL-STOCKED PANTRY

Flavorings

- Kosher salt, coarse sea salt, fine salt
- Black peppercorns
- Onions
- Fresh garlic
- Fresh ginger
- Anchovies or anchovy paste for flavoring pasta sauces and salad dressings
- Dried herbs: bay leaves, dill, crumbled dried sage, thyme, oregano, tarragon, Italian seasoning blend
- Spices: allspice (whole berries or ground), caraway seeds, chili powder, cinnamon sticks, ground cinnamon, coriander seeds, ground coriander, cumin seeds, ground cumin, curry powder, ground ginger, dry mustard, nutmeg, paprika, cayenne pepper, crushed red pepper, turmeric
- Lemons, limes, oranges. The zest is as valuable as the juice. Organic fruit is recommended when you use a lot of zest.
- Granulated sugar
- Brown sugar
- Honey
- Pure maple syrup
- Unsweetened cocoa powder, natural and/or Dutch-processed
- Bittersweet chocolate, semisweet chocolate chips

THE WELL-STOCKED PANTRY

Canned Goods & Bottled Items

- Canned tomatoes, tomato paste
- Reduced-sodium chicken broth, beef broth and/or vegetable broth
- Clam juice
- "Lite" coconut milk for Asian curries and soups
- Canned beans: cannellini beans, great northern beans, chickpeas, black beans, red kidney beans, pinto beans
- Canned lentils
- Chunk light tuna, salmon and sardines

Grains & Legumes

- Whole-wheat flour and whole-wheat pastry flour (Store opened packages in the refrigerator or freezer.)
- All-purpose flour
- Assorted whole-wheat pastas
- Brown rice and instant brown rice
- Pearl barley, quick-cooking barley
- Rolled oats
- Whole-wheat couscous
- Bulgur
- Dried lentils
- Yellow cornmeal
- Plain dry breadcrumbs
- Wild rice

one for protein to avoid cross-contamination. Some cooks even use a full range of colored cutting boards—the yellow one always for onions and garlic (which can leave a lingering flavor that doesn't go well with fruit), the red always for chicken and beef, the blue for fruit... you get the idea.

3. **Knives:** A 2- or 3-inch paring knife and an 8-inch chef's knife. Don't try to buy your knives online or by mail-order, at least not until you've seen them in a store and held them in your hand; it's essential that you get the "feel" of the knife. It should be a natural extension of your arm, its heft and weight commensurate with your own. Buy the best heavy-duty knives you can afford. Cheap, lightweight models make for harder work, slower prep times and even less safety for the cook. We recommend carbon-steel alloy blades, which do not require sharpening as often as nonalloy blades.

4. **Nonstick and stainless-steel skillets:** Small, medium and large skillets in both stainless and nonstick are essential tools for the well-equipped cook. Nonstick cookware is a modern marvel and essential when cooking with little or no fat. There are a few things to keep in mind about the surface. It can be nicked or scratched by metal utensils, rendering it unusable, and it should never be exposed to high heat without ingredients in the pan. Use nonstick pans only when a recipe requires it. Each skillet, ideally, should have a cover, although you can often jury-rig one with a baking sheet or a pot lid.

5. **Saucepans:** Store your stockpot for cooking for crowds; for just the two of you, you'll need a set of saucepans. We prefer multi-ply, stainless-steel, copper-core pots. While they'll set your budget back a notch or two, no amount of fancy cooking techniques can overcome poor-quality cookware.

6. **Bowls:** We love our space-saving, nesting set of three stainless-steel mixing bowls (small, medium and large). Glass or ceramic mixing bowls, while beautiful, chip and break. Stainless-steel bowls are relatively indestructible and have a natural nonstick and nonreactive finish. Lately, we've seen rubber-coated bowls on the market; these are great because they don't slip while you're mixing. And even though you're cooking in smaller quantities it's good to have a big bowl on hand for messy mixing jobs.

7. **A kitchen scale.** Buy a kitchen scale that can be "zeroed out." In other words, you can set a container on it, reset the machine to zero, and then measure the food you add without worrying about subtracting the weight of the container. Using a scale may seem fussy, but think about it: if you have more or less of an ingredient than a recipe calls for, you will throw off the cooking time and taste of the entire dish, not to mention its nutritional profile.

8. **An instant-read thermometer.** The only way to follow recommended temperature guidelines for food safety is to accurately measure the internal temperature of foods. A thermometer with a simple dial gauge, available at

supermarkets, will work as well as a fancy digital one. Sometimes, when you are cooking with thin cuts—a cutlet or cube steak, for example—a thermometer may be hard to use, so visual cues (slicing the chicken to see if it's still pink, for example) are useful.

9. **Spoons:** Two or three wooden spoons for stirring; a plastic or metal slotted spoon for draining.

10. **Colander:** Look for a sturdy one that fits in your sink, stands up well to heat and is easy to clean.

11. **Roasting pan:** A good roasting pan is a heavy, metal pan with a shiny interior surface that holds heat and reflects it back onto the food. Again, think about the size; if you are roasting for two, a pan that fits in a toaster oven is just right. Save that huge one for the Thanksgiving turkey you're cooking for a crowd.

12. **Storage containers:** Of course all cooks need these for leftovers and such, but the cooking-for-two cook will want them for unused ingredients. Many of your needs can be met with resealable plastic freezer bags and by freezing foods in ice cube trays or mini-muffin pans; remove them when frozen and bag them in those freezer bags for later use.

Think Like a Pro

Professional chefs, preparing scores of meals in a single day, have wisdom to offer home cooks.

1. **Change it up.** Change out of any flowing clothing (loose sleeves can catch on fire or get caught in equipment) and take off any excessive jewelry. While you're at it, slip on comfortable shoes and, for those with long locks, tie your hair back. Then pour yourself a glass of sparkling water, fruit juice or wine, and put on your favorite tunes; a composed cook is a more efficient one.

2. **Read the recipe.** Give yourself a minute to imagine doing the steps. There is nothing more aggravating than finding out, 15 minutes before you think you are going to serve dinner, that the dish needs to be refrigerated for 2 hours.

3. **Remember "mise en place."** That's chef-speak (*"meeze-ohn-plahce"*) for having all your ingredients chopped and ready, and your tools clean and available. This includes clean dish towels (for spills and wiping your hands) and oven mitts and trivets (for hot items, and a place to put them). Having everything at your fingertips means the dish will come together faster. That being said, remember that quick cooking is about getting maximal results in a minimal amount of time. If, for instance, a recipe calls for cooking an ingredient first, make use of that cooking time to get some of your other prep work done.

4. **Get a jump on cooking times:** Bring vegetables to room temperature before cooking; you'll find they cook faster. For food-safety reasons, we don't

THE WELL-STOCKED PANTRY

Nuts, Seeds & Fruits

- Walnuts
- Pecans
- Almonds
- Hazelnuts
- Dry-roasted unsalted peanuts
- Pine nuts
- Sesame seeds

  (*Store opened packages of nuts and seeds in the refrigerator or freezer.*)

- Natural peanut butter
- Tahini
- Assorted dried fruits, such as apricots, prunes, cherries, cranberries, dates, figs, raisins

Refrigerator Basics

- Low-fat milk or soymilk
- Low-fat or nonfat plain yogurt and/or vanilla yogurt
- Reduced-fat sour cream
- Good-quality Parmesan cheese and/or Romano cheese
- Sharp Cheddar cheese
- Eggs (large). Keep them on hand for fast omelets and frittatas.
- Orange juice
- Dry white wine. If you wish, substitute nonalcoholic wine.
- Water-packed tofu

Freezer Basics

- Fruit-juice concentrates (orange, apple, pineapple)
- Frozen vegetables: edamame (soybeans), peas, spinach, broccoli, bell pepper and onion mix, corn, chopped onions, small whole onions, uncooked hash browns
- Frozen berries
- Italian turkey sausage and sliced prosciutto to flavor fast pasta sauces
- Low-fat vanilla ice cream or frozen yogurt for impromptu desserts

advocate letting meat, poultry, fish or dairy sit out, but we do know that the room-temperature trick works well with vegetables.

5. **Substitute thoughtfully.** Although some substitutions seem obvious (using onions when you don't have shallots, for example), they can be tricky business. A ruined dish is a waste of time and money, not to mention a huge, hunger-increasing disappointment.

6. **Measure carefully.** Nothing wrecks a quick-cooking sauté like a double portion of salt, while mismeasuring other seasonings may leave a dish over-spiced or bland.

7. **Think big—at least when it comes to bowls.** Ever try making tuna salad in a cereal bowl? Get out the bigger bowls—you'll avoid a mess on the counter, and you won't have to transfer things to bigger bowls once they become unwieldy.

8. **Move the mess… to the sink.** Stir batters, coatings and spice mixtures in bowls set in the sink. Then simply wash any spills down the drain.

9. **Clean as you cook.** This may mean wiping down a dirty counter or stacking some used dishes in the dishwasher while the pasta water boils or the onions sauté. Aim to start and finish with a clean kitchen. And always put each tool back in the same place—so you will know exactly where to find it the next time.

10. **Pay attention.** It turns out that a watched pot always boils, but if you walk away, it may boil down to nothing. All timing guidelines are just that—guidelines—so don't be tempted to set a timer and get on the phone. As you cook, be aware of visual and olfactory cues; if the steak smells like it's starting to burn, it probably is.

Basics of Cooking Techniques

WITH A KNIFE

The way you cut ingredients is important; it helps distribute the ingredient throughout the dish (mincing or finely chopping garlic, for example), ensure that ingredients cook at the same time (like cutting your carrots and potatoes into 1-inch dice) or improve texture (a thinly sliced piece of smoked salmon, for example, is more tempting on your bagel than a fat chunk). Pay attention to, but don't stress about these terms: your common sense will go a long way in helping you as you cook.

Mince and finely chop: "Mincing" is the finest chop of all, less than ⅛ inch, achieved by first cutting, then rocking the knife back and forth across the ingredients, all the while rotating the blade around on the cutting board. "Finely chop" is just a little bit larger than mince.

Chop and coarsely chop: You want to wind up with about a ¼-inch piece when you chop, a bit larger when you "coarsely chop." The idea of chopping (unlike dicing, *below*) is that the ingredients don't have to be strictly uniform in size when you're done.

Dice and cube: You're aiming for uniformity of size here, and it's based on cooking time and texture, not aesthetics. Most recipes that call for a "dice" or "cube" will indicate the preferred size for cooking in the time allotted (e.g., "cut into 1-inch cubes"). Ignore these measurements and you will alter the cooking time.

Slice and thinly slice: "Slice" is a judgment call; a slice of apple will be thinner than a slice of steak, but if you insist on a rule of thumb, think of a slice no thinner than ¼ inch. "Thinly slice," however, means you will want to cut the food as thinly as possible. Again, this will vary by ingredient; you can slice an apple to near-transparent thinness, which is hard to do with steak.

OVER THE HEAT

For the best flavor, heat the oil in a skillet or saucepan before you add the food. Never overcrowd the pan, which fortunately rarely happens when you are cooking for two. Give your skillet or saucepan a shake occasionally to keep ingredients from sticking. Here are terms you will encounter in this book, and others.

Simmer: Set the pan on steady if fairly low heat (thus the constant reminder to "reduce heat" before simmering); you may be instructed to cover or partially cover the pan. Look for some bubbles and steam in the liquid. One reminder: a covered pot will boil more quickly than an uncovered one, so watch the temperature carefully to keep the simmer low and steady.

Braise, stew: These two terms (you can use them interchangeably) are a subset of "simmer," but involve more liquid, a longer cooking time and even lower heat. Braising has traditionally been used for tough cuts of meat (think pot roast).

Stir-fry: A high-heat method of searing meats, poultry, fish and vegetables, usually associated with Asian cooking. You must use oil for stir-frying, otherwise the high temperature will cause the natural sugars to burn and foods to stick to the pan—even a nonstick one.

Steam: Cook a food over moist, high heat, and you preserve many of its otherwise water-soluble nutrients. To steam effectively, you need a pot large enough to hold both the steamer basket and 1 or 2 inches of water with plenty of airflow all around the basket. The food must never sit in the water. Check the water level from time to time to make sure the pan isn't dry, and shake the pan gently once or twice to rearrange the food, ensuring even cooking.

Roast: Whether at a high or low heat, roasting involves a steady, even, dry heat that cooks from the outside in (the opposite of microwaving, which cooks from the inside out). Air (and thus heat) should circulate freely around whatever's being roasted; the oven rack should be placed in the center of the oven unless otherwise stated in the recipe. When roasting vegetables, add a small amount of fat to the pan to sear them while they cook. When roasting meats, a small rack at the bottom of the pan accomplishes two goals: it lifts the meat out of the fat drippings and allows the heat to circulate underneath for even cooking.

Broil: This is an indoor cousin of grilling and sears food with high, direct heat. A broiler should always be preheated for at least 5 minutes; food should be placed so that it (not the broiler pan) is 4 to 6 inches from the heat source. Foods blotted dry broil with less mess. Pour off rendered fat occasionally to avoid flare-ups.

Grill vs. barbecue: If your experience is limited to throwing burgers on a hibachi, it may surprise you to learn that there are actually two methods of cooking on a grill. "Grilling" involves placing ingredients directly over the heat source. "Barbecuing," by contrast, involves putting the food on one side of the grill, the coals or heat source on the other, thereby cooking the food over indirect heat. Experienced grillers test their grills by "feel." Place your open palm 5 inches above the grill grate; the fire is: **high** if you have to move your hand in 2 seconds, **medium** if you have to move your hand in 5 seconds, and **low** if you have to move your hand in 10 seconds.

Basics of Food Safety

SHOPPING

When to shop: If possible, go grocery shopping as your last errand before heading home. If you must run other errands, put a cooler in the car and buy a bag of ice to keep the perishables chilled. In fact, in hotter climates, you need a cooler in the car even if shopping is your last stop. Forty-five minutes in summertime traffic can render meat rancid, milk spoiled and butter liquid.

While you shop: Put meats or fish in plastic bags before you stick them in your cart so they don't drip on the vegetables or pantry items.

STORAGE

Get the perishables in your refrigerator or freezer ASAP. Never store eggs, milk and the like on your refrigerator door, which is the part of the fridge with the greatest temperature fluctuations. We recommend setting your refrigerator temperature control for 40°F, and using the door for storing ketchup, mustard and convenience products that are not so easily subject to spoilage.

Freezing: It's recommended that your freezer be kept at 2°F for safe frozen-food storage.

PREPARING TO COOK

Defrost food in the refrigerator or the microwave to deter bacterial growth. Leaving it out at room temperature to defrost does the opposite.

Before you begin cooking, **wash your hands** with soap under warm water for at least 20 seconds (about as long as it takes to sing the chorus of "Jingle Bells"). **Rinse off fruits and vegetables** under cool running water. But despite what your mother may have taught you, **it's not wise to rinse off poultry, meat or fish**. The bacterial contaminants can only be killed at temperatures above 160°F, far hotter than the hot water in our homes. Rinsing only allows for random splashes—and thus cross-contamination of counters and cabinets.

Unwrap meats and fish in the sink and leave them in their container or paper until you're ready to use them. Immediately throw out the container or paper; never reuse it.

Avoid cross-contamination by having at least two cutting boards, one for the meat or fish and another for fresh produce.

CLEANING UP

Wash plastic cutting boards in the dishwasher; wash your knives in hot, soapy water. And wash your counters with hot, soapy water. An occasional thorough once-over with a kitchen disinfectant spray is a good idea.

Pattern for Health

What does a healthy eating pattern look like? One simple visualization winning praise across the board is the "Divide Your Plate" strategy.

● Imagine a dinner plate and divide it in half.

● Fill one half with vegetables and divide the other half into two quarters.

● Fill one quarter with lean protein, such as fish, skinless poultry, lean beef, beans or tofu.

● Fill the other quarter with a grain-based or starchy side dish, preferably a whole grain like brown rice, whole-wheat pasta or a slice of whole-grain bread.

What this method lacks in precision it more than makes up for in good sense. If you focus on making most of your meals look this way, you'll automatically be following sound nutrition guidelines and choosing appropriate portions—without having to pull out a nutrition guide or a measuring cup every time.

Remember That Eating Well Means:

● Selecting a variety of foods in sensible portions

● Considering no food either a magic bullet or a forbidden fruit

● Choosing whole foods over processed ones as often as possible

● Embracing plant foods like vegetables, fruits, beans and whole grains

● Including low-fat dairy products, fish and shellfish, lean meats and poultry

● Relying on seasoning and cooking dishes with olive oil and the other "good fats" that make food tastier and more satisfying, while keeping a watchful eye on saturated fat and trans fat.

But most of all, eating well means eating with pleasure—in a relaxed and friendly environment. Enjoy every bite!

Menu Suggestions

NEW YEAR'S EVE CELEBRATION FOR TWO

Salt & Pepper Shrimp (*page 179*)

Rice noodles

Fresh fruit sorbet with fortune cookies

SUPER BOWL FOR TWO

Fresh cut-up vegetables with
   Buttermilk Ranch Dressing
   (*page 225*)

White Chili (*page 62*)

Cornbread

Pineapple-Coconut Frappe (*page 241*)

VALENTINE'S DINNER

Pomegranate Duck (*page 139*)

Herbed Whole-Wheat Couscous
   (*page 228*)

Sautéed Watercress (*page 232*)

Strawberries, mango slices, orange
   segments and cubes of reduced-fat
   pound cake to dip in
   Chocolate Sauce (*page 240*)

HOT DATE

**Pork Chops with Maple-Mustard
   Sauce** (*page 203*)

Braised baby artichokes (*page 233*)

Wild Rice Salad (*page 228*)

Marsala-Poached Figs over Ricotta
   (*page 241*)

STUDY BREAK

Lentil & Chicken Stew (*page 58*)

Garlic-Tomato Toasts (*page 229*)

Old-Fashioned Fruit Crumble (*page 241*)

BREAKFAST FOR DINNER

**Smoked Trout Hash with
   Mustard Greens** (*page 170*)

Poached eggs

Whole-grain toast

Baked Apples (*page 240*)

ANNIVERSARY

Herb-Coated Filet Mignon (*page 193*)

Buttermilk-Herb Mashed Potatoes
   (*page 229*)

Orange-Infused Green Beans &
   Red Pepper (*page 231*)

Bananas in Brown Sugar-Rum Sauce
   (*page 240*)

VEGETARIAN

Eggplant-Cheddar Bake (*page 102*)

Whole-wheat pasta

Balsamic-Vinegar Spiked Strawberries
   (*page 240*)

Crispy Seitan Stir-Fry (*page 108*)

Brown rice (*page 239*)

Roasted Grapes (*page 242*)

**Creamy Gorgonzola Polenta with
   Summer Squash Sauté** (*page 99*)

Orange & Avocado Salad (*page 227*)

Toasted Pound Cake with Lemon
   Sauce (*page 243*)

Indian-Spiced Kale & Chickpeas
   (*page 101*)

Whole-wheat couscous (*page 239*)

Fruit sorbet

PIZZA NIGHT

Corn & Tomato Pizzas (*page 96*)

The Wedge (*page 228*)

Seared Polenta with Chunky Blueberry
   Sauce (*page 242*)

CINCO DE MAYO

**Chicken Tacos with Charred
   Tomatoes** (*page 128*)

Spiced Pinto Beans (*page 232*)

Raspberry-Mango Sundaes (*page 242*)

SPRING

**Spring Salad with Tarragon
   Vinaigrette** (*page 39*)

Whole-grain baguette

Fresh Fruit with Lemon-Mint Cream
   (*page 240*)

SUMMER

**Marjoram-Rubbed Pork &
   Grilled Potato Salad** (*page 211*)

Sautéed zucchini and summer squash
   (*page 237*)

Stuffed Nectarines (*page 243*)

FALL

Lamb, Fig & Olive Stew (*page 72*)
   served over barley (*page 239*)

Sautéed Pear Sundaes (*page 242*)

WINTER

**Fennel-Crusted Sirloin Tips with
   Bell Peppers** (*page 198*)

Wild rice (*page 239*)

Quick "Cheesecake" (*page 241*)

CHAPTER 1

Dinner Salads

Warm Arugula Salad with Chicken & Chèvre

Grown-up and sophisticated, this salad will make you happy you're not a finicky kid. For an even dressier spin, substitute boneless skinless duck breasts for the chicken.

6   **cups arugula, tough stems removed**
4   **green olives, pitted and quartered**
4   **large dates, pitted and quartered**
1   **orange, peeled, sectioned and sliced into chunks**
¼   **cup seasoned Italian breadcrumbs**
8   **ounces chicken tenders**
2   **teaspoons extra-virgin olive oil**
2   **tablespoons frozen orange juice concentrate, thawed**
1   **tablespoon water**
1   **tablespoon cider vinegar**
1   **tablespoon Dijon mustard**
⅛   **teaspoon salt**
    Freshly ground pepper to taste
⅓   **cup crumbled aged *or* fresh goat cheese (*see Note*)**

1. ♦ Place arugula, olives, dates and orange chunks in a large salad bowl.

2. ♦ Place breadcrumbs on a large plate; roll chicken in the breadcrumbs to coat. Heat oil in a large nonstick skillet over medium-high heat. Add the chicken and cook until golden and just cooked through, 2 to 3 minutes per side. Transfer to a plate; cover and keep warm.

3. ♦ Add orange juice concentrate, water and vinegar to the pan. Stir in mustard and let dressing boil for 30 seconds. Add salt and season with pepper to taste. Add half of the warm dressing to the salad; toss gently to mix.

4. ♦ Divide the salad between 2 plates. Cut the chicken into thin slices. Top each salad with the chicken, goat cheese and remaining dressing.

MAKES **2** SERVINGS.

Active Minutes: **40**

Total: 40 minutes

Per Serving: 379 calories; 15 g fat (6 g sat, 7 g mono); 89 mg cholesterol; 27 g carbohydrate; 36 g protein; 3 g fiber; 654 mg sodium; 483 mg potassium.

Nutrition Bonus: Vitamin C (100% daily value), Vitamin A (40% dv), Calcium (35% dv), Folate (25% dv).

Ingredient Note:

● Goat cheese, also know as *chèvre* (the French word for goat), is earthy-tasting and slightly tart. Fresh goat cheese is creamy and widely available; aged goat cheese has a nutty, sharp flavor and is drier and firmer in texture. Look for aged goat cheese in a well-stocked cheese section at larger markets and specialty cheese shops.

Spinach & Beet Salad
with Chicken

Real maple syrup—not the "maple-flavored" fakes that line the super-market shelves—is the key to the richly flavored dressing on this elegant salad. In this case, the darker the syrup the better; choose Grade B syrup if it's available or the darkest Grade A that you can find.

Active Minutes: **30**

Total: 30 minutes

Per Serving: 364 calories; 24 g fat (4 g sat, 7 g mono); 50 mg cholesterol; 16 g carbohydrate; 22 g protein; 3 g fiber; 631 mg sodium; 644 mg potassium.

Nutrition Bonus: Vitamin A (120% daily value), Folate (36% dv), Vitamin C (35% dv), Iron (25% dv), Potassium (18% dv).

Lower ⬇ **Carbs**

Tip:

● To toast chopped pecans or walnuts, cook in a small dry skillet over medium-low heat, stirring constantly, until fragrant and lightly browned, 2 to 4 minutes.

8	**ounces boneless, skinless chicken breast, trimmed of fat**
2	**tablespoons walnut *or* canola oil**
1	**tablespoon maple syrup**
1	**tablespoon cider vinegar**
1½	**teaspoons coarse-grained mustard**
1½	**teaspoons reduced-sodium soy sauce**
⅛	**teaspoon salt**
⅛	**teaspoon freshly ground pepper**
4	**cups baby spinach**
1	**8-ounce can whole beets, drained and quartered**
¼	**cup crumbled goat cheese**
2	**tablespoons chopped pecans, toasted (*see Tip*)**

1. Place chicken in a small skillet or saucepan and add enough water to cover; bring to a simmer over high heat. Cover, reduce heat and simmer gently until the chicken is cooked through and no longer pink in the middle, 10 to 12 minutes. Transfer the chicken to a cutting board. When cool enough to handle, cut into ¼-inch-thick slices.

2. Meanwhile, whisk oil, syrup, vinegar, mustard, soy sauce, salt and pepper in a large bowl. Reserve 2 tablespoons of the dressing in a small bowl. Add spinach to the large bowl; toss to coat with dressing. Divide the spinach between 2 plates, top with the chicken, beets, goat cheese and pecans. Drizzle with the reserved dressing.

MAKES **2** SERVINGS.

Warm Winter Salad

Think outside the (ice)box and serve a warm salad for a delicious change. It's simple to make and a great way to add variety to your salad repertoire. Full of hearty flavors, this is perfect wintertime food.

8 ounces boneless, skinless chicken breast, trimmed of fat
1 tablespoon extra-virgin olive oil
1 pear, sliced
1 small shallot, minced
3 tablespoons sherry vinegar
2 teaspoons Dijon mustard
1 small head radicchio, thinly sliced
1 small fennel bulb, cored and thinly sliced
1 large carrot, cut into matchsticks
1 tablespoon chopped walnuts, toasted (*see Tip, page 26*)
⅛ teaspoon salt, or to taste
⅛ teaspoon freshly ground pepper, or to taste
6 large butterhead lettuce leaves
¼ cup crumbled Gorgonzola *or* goat cheese

Active Minutes: **35**

Total: 35 minutes

Per Serving: 395 calories; 17 g fat (5 g sat, 7 g mono); 75 mg cholesterol; 32 g carbohydrate; 31 g protein; 8 g fiber; 548 mg sodium; 1,058 mg potassium.

Nutrition Bonus: Vitamin A (140% daily value), Vitamin C (40% dv), Potassium (30% dv), Calcium (20% dv), Folate (19% dv).

High ⬆ Fiber

1. Poach chicken (*see Tip, page 245*). Use 2 forks to shred into bite-size pieces.

2. Heat oil in a large nonstick skillet over medium-high heat. Add pear slices and cook, stirring occasionally, until they start to brown, about 2 minutes. Transfer to a small bowl.

3. Whisk shallot, vinegar and mustard in a small bowl; add to the pan and cook, stirring constantly, for 30 seconds. Add the cooked chicken, radicchio, fennel, carrot and walnuts. Cook, stirring occasionally, until just wilted, about 3 minutes. Return the pears to the pan. Season with salt and pepper.

4. Divide lettuce leaves between 2 plates. Top with the warm chicken salad and sprinkle with cheese.

MAKES **2** SERVINGS.

Coconut-Lime Chicken & Snow Peas

Double the flavor, halve the work—simply by using the same tangy combination of coconut milk, lime juice and brown sugar for both poaching the chicken and dressing the salad. Crisp romaine lettuce, cabbage and snow peas add freshness and an irresistible crunch.

1 cup "lite" coconut milk (*see Tips for Two*)
¼ cup lime juice
2 tablespoons brown sugar
½ teaspoon salt
8 ounces chicken tenders
4 cups shredded romaine lettuce
1 cup shredded red cabbage
1 cup sliced snow peas
3 tablespoons minced fresh cilantro
2 tablespoons minced red onion

1. Preheat oven to 400°F.

2. Whisk coconut milk, lime juice, brown sugar and salt in an 8-inch-square glass baking dish. Transfer ¼ cup of the dressing to a large bowl; set aside.

3. Place chicken in the baking dish; bake until cooked through, about 20 minutes.

4. Meanwhile, add lettuce, cabbage, snow peas, cilantro and onion to the large bowl with the dressing; toss to coat. Divide between 2 plates.

5. Transfer the chicken to a cutting board and thinly slice. Arrange the chicken slices on top of the salads. Drizzle 1 tablespoon of the cooking liquid over each of the salads.

MAKES 2 SERVINGS.

Active Minutes: **35**

Total: 35 minutes

To Make Ahead: The dressing (Step 2) will keep for up to 2 days.

Per Serving: 186 calories; 3 g fat (1 g sat, 0 g mono); 67 mg cholesterol; 14 g carbohydrate; 29 g protein; 4 g fiber; 191 mg sodium; 473 mg potassium.

Nutrition Bonus: Vitamin A (140% daily value), Vitamin C (120% dv), Folate (40% dv), Iron (15% dv).

Healthy)(Weight

Lower ⬇ Carbs

Tips for Two
COCONUT MILK

STORAGE: Refrigerate for up to 4 days or freeze for up to 2 months.
USES: Make extra Coconut-Lime Dressing; drizzle on sliced fresh fruit; use as some of the liquid for cooking rice; Pineapple-Coconut Frappe (*page 241*).

EatingWell Cobb Salad

Legend has it that in 1937 Bob Cobb, owner of Hollywood's Brown Derby restaurant, invented this combination from leftovers he found in the fridge (with some bacon swiped from a busy chef). Our version is fairly true to the original, although many would argue that the blue cheese should never be "optional"; we've labeled it as such for those who don't care for its flavor or the extra calories. Warm up a crusty whole-grain baguette, pour a crisp, cold glass of sparkling wine and dig in.

Active Minutes: **40**

Total: **40 minutes**

Per Serving: 207 calories; 13 g fat (2 g sat, 8 g mono); 93 mg cholesterol; 6 g carbohydrate; 18 g protein; 3 g fiber; 312 mg sodium; 511 mg potassium.

Nutrition Bonus: Vitamin A (30% daily value), Vitamin C (25% dv).

Healthy ⋈ **Weight**

Lower ⬇ **Carbs**

Tip:

- To poach chicken breasts, place boneless, skinless breasts in a medium skillet or saucepan and add enough water to cover; bring to a boil. Cover, reduce heat to low and simmer gently until the chicken is cooked through and no longer pink in the middle, 10 to 12 minutes.

- 2 tablespoons white-wine vinegar
- 1 tablespoon finely minced shallot
- 2 teaspoons Dijon mustard
- ¼ teaspoon salt
- ½ teaspoon freshly ground pepper
- 4 teaspoons extra-virgin olive oil
- 1 5-ounce bag mixed salad greens (about 5 cups)
- 6 ounces shredded cooked chicken breast (about 1 medium breast; *see Tip*)
- 1 large hard-boiled egg (*see Tip, page 244*), peeled and chopped
- 1 strip bacon, cooked and crumbled
- 1 medium tomato, diced
- 1 small cucumber, seeded and sliced
- ½ avocado, diced
- ¼ cup crumbled blue cheese (optional)

1. Whisk vinegar, shallot, mustard, salt and pepper in a small bowl to combine. Whisk in oil until combined. Place salad greens in a large bowl. Add half of the dressing; toss to coat.

2. Divide the salad greens between 2 plates. Arrange equal portions of chicken, egg, bacon, tomato, cucumber, avocado and blue cheese (if using) on top of the salad greens. Drizzle the salads with the remaining dressing.

MAKES **2** SERVINGS.

Madras Chicken & Broccoli Salad

Curry powder and mango chutney are the flavor-intensive secret ingredients in this swift and simple Indian-inspired salad. If you want, double this recipe and you'll have a great lunch for the next day.

Active Minutes: **20**

Total: 30 minutes

Per Serving: 266 calories; 9 g fat (2 g sat, 4 g mono); 61 mg cholesterol; 19 g carbohydrate; 29 g protein; 3 g fiber; 222 mg sodium; 555 mg potassium.

Nutrition Bonus: Vitamin C (120% daily value), Vitamin A (50% dv), Magnesium (21% dv), Potassium (16% dv).

Healthy)(Weight

Lower ⬇ Carbs

8	ounces boneless, skinless chicken breast, trimmed of fat
1/3	cup nonfat plain yogurt
1	tablespoon prepared mango chutney (*see Tips for Two*)
1	teaspoon hot Madras curry powder
2	tablespoons chopped fresh cilantro
2	cups finely chopped broccoli
1/4	cup finely chopped red onion
1/4	cup chopped cashews

1. Place chicken in a small skillet or saucepan and add enough water to cover; bring to a boil. Cover, reduce heat to low and simmer gently until the chicken is cooked through and no longer pink in the middle, 10 to 12 minutes. Transfer to a cutting board, cut into 1/2-inch cubes and cool to room temperature.

2. Meanwhile, whisk yogurt, chutney, curry and cilantro in a medium bowl until thoroughly combined. Add broccoli, onion, cashews and the cooked chicken; toss to coat.

MAKES **2** SERVINGS.

Tips for Two

MANGO CHUTNEY

STORAGE: Refrigerate for up to 6 months.

USES: Whisk with yogurt for a quick dressing, dip or marinade; serve alongside grilled meat, fish or chicken; blend with reduced-fat cream cheese for a zingy spread.

Captiva Shrimp & Chicken Salad

Mango—diced and pureed—gives chicken and shrimp a tropical flavor jolt. But don't be upset that the recipe only uses half a mango; that leaves some for tonight's dessert or tomorrow's breakfast (eat it plain or stir it into yogurt). Better yet, blend it into a margarita (virgin or not) to enjoy with your meal.

4	ounces boneless, skinless chicken breast, trimmed of fat
½	small mango, diced (*see Tip, page 244*), divided
¾	teaspoon freshly grated lime zest
1	tablespoon lime juice
1½	teaspoons extra-virgin olive oil
1½	teaspoons dark rum
	Several dashes of hot sauce, to taste
¾	teaspoon chopped fresh mint *or* ¼ teaspoon dried
1	small clove garlic, peeled
¼	teaspoon salt
2	cups fresh spinach, trimmed and cut into ½-inch strips
4	ounces cooked, peeled shrimp (31-35 per pound)

1. Place chicken in a small skillet or saucepan and add enough water to cover; bring to a boil. Cover, reduce heat to low and simmer gently until the chicken is cooked through and no longer pink in the middle, 10 to 12 minutes. Transfer to a cutting board and use 2 forks to shred into bite-size pieces. Chill in a medium bowl in the refrigerator while preparing the rest of the salad.

2. Place 2 tablespoons mango, lime zest and juice, oil, rum, hot sauce, mint, garlic and salt in a blender or food processor; process until smooth.

3. Add spinach, shrimp and the remaining mango to the cooked chicken. Add the dressing and toss gently to combine.

MAKES **2** SERVINGS.

Active Minutes: **30**

Total: 30 minutes

To Make Ahead: Prepare the dressing (Step 2), cover and refrigerate for up to 8 hours.

Per Serving: 232 calories; 6 g fat (1 g sat, 3 g mono); 152 mg cholesterol; 13 g carbohydrate; 29 g protein; 2 g fiber; 518 mg sodium; 528 mg potassium.

Nutrition Bonus: Vitamin A (70% daily value), Vitamin C (50% dv), Folate (17% dv), Potassium (15% dv).

Healthy ⚖ Weight

Lower ⬇ Carbs

Caesar Salad Three Ways

Light and lemony, our version of the classic Caesar salad lets the taste of the greens and salmon shine through. If you prefer, shrimp or chicken can be substituted for the salmon (see variations).

Active Minutes: **25**

Total: 25 minutes

To Make Ahead: The dressing will keep in the refrigerator for up to 3 days.

Per Serving: 483 calories; 32 g fat (7 g sat, 15 g mono); 79 mg cholesterol; 17 g carbohydrate; 29 g protein; 1 g fiber; 650 mg sodium; 440 mg potassium.

Nutrition Bonus: Selenium & Vitamin C (60% daily value), Vitamin A (50% dv), high omega-3s.

Lower ⬇ Carbs

Caesar Salad Dressing (*page 225*)
2   **teaspoons extra-virgin olive oil**
8   **ounces skinned salmon fillet (*see Tip, page 245*) *or* peeled and deveined shrimp (21-25 per pound) *or* chicken tenders**
4   **cups chopped hearts of romaine (about 1 heart)**
½   **cup croutons, preferably whole-grain (*see Tip*)**
2   **tablespoons shaved Asiago cheese (*see Tip, page 245*)**
2   **lemon wedges for garnish**

1. ◆ Prepare Caesar Salad Dressing. Place in a large bowl.

2. ◆ Heat oil in a medium nonstick skillet over medium-high heat until shimmering but not smoking. Cook salmon, skinned-side up, until golden brown, 3 to 6 minutes. Turn the salmon over and remove the pan from the heat. Allow the salmon to finish cooking off the heat until just cooked through, 3 to 6 minutes more. Divide the salmon into 2 portions.

3. ◆ Add romaine and croutons to the dressing and toss to coat. Divide the salad between 2 plates, top with the salmon and Asiago. Garnish with lemon wedges.

MAKES **2** SERVINGS.

Croutons:

● To make your own: Toss ½ cup whole-grain bread cubes with 1 ½ teaspoons extra-virgin olive oil, a pinch each of salt, pepper and garlic powder. Spread out on a baking sheet and toast at 350°F until crispy, turning occasionally, 15 to 20 minutes.

Shrimp Variation:

In Step 2, substitute shrimp for the salmon. Heat 1 teaspoon olive oil in the skillet over medium-high heat. Add shrimp in a single layer and cook, turning once, until pink and curled, about 2 minutes per side.

Chicken Variation:

In Step 2, substitute chicken tenders for the salmon. Heat 1 teaspoon oil in the skillet over medium-high heat. Add chicken and cook, turning once, until cooked through, 2 to 3 minutes per side.

Seared Tuna & Watercress with Scallion-Ginger Relish

Here's a salad that's as beautiful as it is delicious. The spicy orange-ginger dressing is so good, you'll want to double (or triple) it to serve on your salads throughout the week.

2	tablespoons orange juice
1	tablespoon reduced-sodium soy sauce
1	tablespoon toasted sesame oil
1	teaspoon minced fresh ginger
1/2	teaspoon hot sauce
1/4	teaspoon freshly ground pepper, divided
1/2	cup thinly sliced scallions
1/2	cup drained, canned water chestnuts, diced (*see Tips for Two*)
1	tablespoon sesame seeds, toasted (*see Tip, page 245*)
1	8-ounce tuna steak, about 1 inch thick
1/2	teaspoon canola oil
1/8	teaspoon salt
4	cups watercress, washed and trimmed (about 1 bunch)

1. Preheat grill to medium-high heat.

2. Combine orange juice, soy sauce, sesame oil, ginger, hot sauce and 1/8 teaspoon pepper in a large bowl. To prepare scallion-ginger relish: transfer half the dressing to a small bowl; add scallions, water chestnuts and sesame seeds, and toss.

3. Rub tuna with canola oil and sprinkle with salt and the remaining 1/8 teaspoon pepper. Grill until the fish is opaque, 4 to 5 minutes per side.

4. Add watercress to the large bowl and toss to coat with the remaining dressing. Cut the tuna into 2 portions. Divide the watercress between 2 plates and top with the tuna and scallion-ginger relish.

MAKES **2** SERVINGS.

Active Minutes: **45**

Total: 45 minutes

To Make Ahead: Prepare the relish (Step 2), cover and refrigerate for up to 6 hours.

Per Serving: 313 calories; 16 g fat (3 g sat, 6 g mono); 43 mg cholesterol; 12 g carbohydrate; 30 g protein; 3 g fiber; 543 mg sodium; 603 mg potassium.

Nutrition Bonus: Vitamin A (110% daily value), Vitamin C (60% dv), Iron (45% dv), Potassium (17% dv).

Healthy))(Weight

Lower ⬇ Carbs

Tips for Two
WATER CHESTNUTS
STORAGE: Store in the refrigerator, covered with water; they keep for up to 1 month with daily water changes.
USES: Add to a stir-fry; toss in a green salad; jazz up chicken or tuna salad; Asian Brown Rice (*page 228*).

Tuna & Red Pepper Antipasto

Packed with protein and fiber, this tasty salad is ready in a flash. Serve on a bed of lettuce with warm, crusty bread or pack it in a pita for a sandwich. For an extra kick, add a pinch of crushed red pepper or cayenne.

- 1 **15-ounce can beans, such as kidney beans, black-eyed peas *or* fava beans, rinsed**
- 1 **small red bell pepper, finely diced, *or* one 7-ounce jar roasted red peppers, rinsed and diced**
- 1 **3-ounce can chunk light tuna, drained and flaked**
- 1/4 **cup finely chopped red onion**
- 2 **tablespoons lemon juice**
- 2 **tablespoons chopped fresh parsley**
- 1 **tablespoon extra-virgin olive oil**
- 2 **teaspoons capers, rinsed**
- 3/4 **teaspoon finely chopped fresh rosemary**
- 1/8 **teaspoon salt**
  Freshly ground pepper to taste

Active Minutes: **15**

Total: 15 minutes

Per Serving: 304 calories; 8 g fat (1 g sat, 5 g mono); 27 mg cholesterol; 36 g carbohydrate; 23 g protein; 14 g fiber; 686 mg sodium; 643 mg potassium.

Nutrition Bonus: Vitamin C (140% daily value), Vitamin A (30% dv), Folate (29% dv), Potassium (18% dv).

High ⬆ Fiber

I Place beans, bell pepper, tuna, onion, lemon juice, parsley, oil, capers and rosemary in a medium bowl; stir to combine. Season with salt and pepper.

MAKES **2** SERVINGS.

Spring Salad with Tarragon Vinaigrette

A bold, layered salad that showcases sardines and asparagus, this beautiful dish adds variety to your weekday dining. If you prefer tuna to sardines or have fish from the night before, go ahead and use that instead.

- **2 tablespoons red-wine vinegar**
- **2 tablespoons extra-virgin olive oil**
- **1 teaspoon whole-grain mustard**
- **¼ teaspoon dried tarragon**
- **Pinch of salt**
- **Pinch of freshly ground pepper**
- **1 clove garlic, crushed**
- **½ bunch asparagus, tough ends trimmed**
- **2 large hard-boiled eggs (*see Tip, page 244*)**
- **1 5-ounce bag mixed salad greens (about 5 cups)**
- **10 cherry tomatoes**
- **1 4-ounce can sardines, drained**
- **6 olives (optional)**

1. Whisk vinegar, oil, mustard, tarragon, salt and pepper in a small bowl. Add garlic and set aside.

2. Bring 1 inch of water to a boil in a medium skillet. Add asparagus, stirring to submerge if necessary, and cook until bright green and crisp-tender, about 3 minutes. Drain and place under cold running water until cooled.

3. Peel and slice eggs. Divide salad greens between 2 plates and top with the eggs, asparagus, tomatoes, sardines and olives (if using). Remove the garlic from the dressing, stir to combine and drizzle over the salads.

MAKES **2** SERVINGS.

Active Minutes: **20**

Total: 30 minutes

To Make Ahead: Hard-boil the eggs and refrigerate for up to 4 days.

Per Serving: 360 calories; 26 g fat (5 g sat, 15 g mono); 287 mg cholesterol; 9 g carbohydrate; 23 g protein; 4 g fiber; 485 mg sodium; 846 mg potassium.

Nutrition Bonus: Vitamin A (70% daily value), Vitamin C (45% dv), Calcium (30% dv), Iron (20% dv).

Lower ⬇ Carbs

Marinated Mussel Salad

Archaeologists say that humans have been eating mussels for over 20,000 years, but it's unlikely our prehistoric ancestors ever tried them with this tangy lemon-caper marinade. Garlic-Tomato Toasts (*page 229*) and a bold Sauvignon Blanc are wonderful with this salad.

Active Minutes: **30**

Total: **30 minutes**

To Make Ahead: Prepare through Step 2. Cover and chill for up to 8 hours.

Per Serving: **204 calories; 9 g fat (1 g sat, 4 g mono); 48 mg cholesterol; 9 g carbohydrate; 21 g protein; 1 g fiber; 372 mg sodium; 363 mg potassium.**

Nutrition Bonus: Vitamin A (90% daily value), Vitamin C (40% dv), Iron (35% dv), Folate (22% dv).

Healthy)(Weight

Lower ⬇ Carbs

2	**pounds mussels, debearded and scrubbed (*see Tip*)**
1	**medium onion, chopped**
1	**cup water**
1	**cup dry white wine**
2	**tablespoons lemon juice**
1	**tablespoon chopped fresh parsley**
2	**teaspoons extra-virgin olive oil**
1	**teaspoon capers, rinsed**
1/4	**teaspoon dry mustard**
	Freshly ground pepper to taste
4	**cups torn leaf lettuce, such as Boston, red leaf *or* romaine**

1. Place mussels, onion, water and wine in a large saucepan. Cover and bring to a boil over high heat. Cook just until the mussels open, 2 to 3 minutes. Drain, cool and shell the mussels, discarding any that do not open.

2. Combine lemon juice, parsley, oil, capers, mustard and pepper in a medium bowl. Add the shelled mussels; marinate for at least 5 minutes.

3. To serve, divide lettuce between 2 plates and top with the mussel mixture.

MAKES **2** SERVINGS.

Tip:

● Use a stiff brush to scrub mussels under running water. Discard any with broken shells or any whose shells remain open after you tap them lightly. Scrape off any barnacles; pull off the black fibrous "beard" (*see photo, page 244*).

Southeast Asian Scallops & Greens

F resh herbs and Asian flavors add interest to meaty sea scallops. Grilled steak or chicken can easily be substituted for the scallops; or, for a truly quick preparation, use precooked shrimp.

3 tablespoons rice vinegar

2 tablespoons lime juice

1 tablespoon toasted sesame oil

2 teaspoons minced fresh ginger

2 teaspoons reduced-sodium soy sauce

8 ounces dry sea scallops (*see Note*)

1/8 teaspoon kosher salt

1/8 teaspoon freshly ground pepper

4 cups mixed salad greens, preferably baby Asian greens

1 small red bell pepper, diced

1/2 cup assorted fresh herb leaves, such as basil, cilantro and/or mint

2 teaspoons sesame seeds, toasted (*see Tip, page 245*)

1. Preheat grill to medium-high.

2. Whisk vinegar, lime juice, oil, ginger and soy sauce in a medium bowl.

3. Thread scallops onto two 12-inch skewers. Sprinkle with salt and pepper. Oil the grill rack (*see Tip, page 244*). Grill the scallops until cooked through, about 4 minutes per side. Carefully remove the scallops from the skewers.

4. Add salad greens, bell pepper and herbs to the dressing; toss to combine. Serve the salad topped with the scallops and sesame seeds.

MAKES 2 SERVINGS.

Active Minutes: **25**

Total: 25 minutes

Per Serving: 221 calories; 10 g fat (1 g sat, 3 g mono); 37 mg cholesterol; 12 g carbohydrate; 22 g protein; 4 g fiber; 463 mg sodium; 887 mg potassium.

Nutrition Bonus: Vitamin C (160% daily value), Vitamin A (100% dv), Iron (40% dv), Selenium (36% dv).

Healthy)(Weight

Lower Carbs

Ingredient Note:

- Be sure to buy "dry" scallops, which have not been treated with sodium tripolyphosphate (STP). They are more flavorful and will brown properly.

Tex-Mex Taco Salad

This version of the chain-restaurant favorite has fresh flavors and a healthy nutritional profile. Vary the heat by varying the type of salsa you use. Baked corn tortilla chips and lime wedges are natural accompaniments.

- ½ **cup prepared salsa**
- 2 **tablespoons reduced-fat sour cream**
- ½ **teaspoon canola oil**
- 1 **small onion, chopped**
- 2 **cloves garlic, minced**
- 8 **ounces lean ground beef** *or* **turkey**
- 1 **large plum tomato, diced**
- ½ **cup canned kidney beans, rinsed (*see Tips for Two*)**
- 1 **teaspoon ground cumin**
- 1 **teaspoon chili powder**
- ⅛ **teaspoon salt, or to taste**
- 2 **tablespoons chopped fresh cilantro**
- 4 **cups shredded romaine lettuce**
- ¼ **cup shredded sharp Cheddar cheese**

Active Minutes: **30**

Total: 30 minutes

Per Serving: 343 calories; 13 g fat (5 g sat, 3 g mono); 81 mg cholesterol; 26 g carbohydrate; 32 g protein; 8 g fiber; 851 mg sodium; 737 mg potassium.

Nutrition Bonus: **Vitamin A (150% daily value), Vitamin C (70% dv), Zinc (30% dv), Iron (25% dv), Potassium (21% dv).**

Healthy ⋈ Weight

High ⬆ Fiber

1. Combine salsa and sour cream in a large bowl.

2. Heat oil in a medium nonstick skillet over medium heat. Add onion and garlic and cook, stirring often, until softened, 1 to 2 minutes. Add beef (or turkey) and cook, stirring often, until cooked through, 3 to 5 minutes. Add tomato, beans, cumin, chili powder and salt; cook, stirring, until the tomato begins to break down, about 2 minutes. Remove from the heat, stir in cilantro and 2 tablespoons of the salsa mixture.

3. Add lettuce to the remaining salsa mixture and toss to coat. Divide the lettuce between 2 plates, top with the cooked meat and sprinkle with cheese.

MAKES **2** SERVINGS.

Tips for Two
CANNED BEANS
STORAGE: Refrigerate for up to 3 days.

USES: Toss with a green salad or into soup for extra protein; mash with garlic powder and chopped fresh herbs for a quick dip; Spiced Pinto Beans (*page 232*).

Grilled Sirloin Salad

This flavorful combo uses only one bowl and the grill; cleanup couldn't be any easier. Choose the greens you like best to give the salad customized character. Serve with grilled baguette, topped with sun-dried tomato tapenade, and icy cold beer.

Active Minutes: **35**

Total: **35 minutes**

Per Serving: 246 calories; 8 g fat (2 g sat, 3 g mono); 47 mg cholesterol; 16 g carbohydrate; 30 g protein; 6 g fiber; 518 mg sodium; 1,099 mg potassium.

Nutrition Bonus: Vitamin C (160% daily value), Vitamin A (120% dv), Potassium (31% dv), Iron & Zinc (30% dv).

Healthy)|(**Weight**

Lower ⬇ **Carbs**

High ⬆ **Fiber**

- 1 **tablespoon reduced-sodium soy sauce**
- 1 **tablespoon balsamic vinegar**
- 1 **teaspoon toasted sesame oil**
- 1 **teaspoon brown sugar**
- ½ **teaspoon finely chopped fresh ginger**
- 1 **clove garlic, peeled and smashed**
- ½ **teaspoon coarsely ground pepper**
- 8 **ounces sirloin steak, trimmed of fat**
- ⅛ **teaspoon salt**
- 8 **scallions, white part only**
- ½ **red bell pepper, seeded**
- 6 **cups torn salad greens, such as escarole, curly endive, radicchio *and/or* watercress**

1. Preheat grill to high. Whisk soy sauce, vinegar, oil, sugar, ginger and garlic in a large bowl until the sugar dissolves.

2. Rub pepper into both sides of steak. Season with salt. Place the steak, scallions and bell pepper half on the grill and cook for 4 minutes. Turn the steak and vegetables and cook until the steak is medium-rare and the vegetables are slightly charred, 3 to 4 minutes more.

3. Let the steak stand for 5 minutes before cutting it, against the grain, into very thin slices. Cut the scallions into 1-inch pieces. Slice the bell pepper into long strips.

4. Toss salad greens with the dressing. Divide between 2 plates and top with the steak and vegetables.

MAKES **2** SERVINGS.

Sweet & Salty Beef Salad

Here's a salad that showcases the Asian yin and yang philosophy of combining opposing flavors. Mild, crisp iceberg lettuce allows the exotic hot-sweet-sour-salty flavors of the warm dressing to shine.

Active Minutes: **35**

Total: **35 minutes**

Per Serving: 337 calories; 12 g fat (3 g sat, 6 g mono); 47 mg cholesterol; 28 g carbohydrate; 30 g protein; 4 g fiber; 585 mg sodium; 735 mg potassium.

Nutrition Bonus: Vitamin C (70% daily value), Zinc (30% dv), Vitamin A (20% dv), Iron (15% dv).

Healthy ✳ Weight

Ingredient Note:

● Fish sauce is a pungent Southeast Asian sauce made from salted, fermented fish. It can be found in the Asian section of large supermarkets and in Asian specialty markets.

1 ½   **tablespoons fish sauce (*see Note*) or reduced-sodium soy sauce**
1 ½   **tablespoons brown sugar**
 ½   **head iceberg lettuce, halved, cored and thinly sliced**
 2   **teaspoons canola oil, divided**
 8   **ounces sirloin steak, trimmed of fat and thinly sliced**
 1   **jalapeño *or* serrano pepper, seeded and minced**
 1   **small onion, finely chopped**
 1   **clove garlic, minced**
 1   **orange, peel and white pith removed (*see Tip, page 245*), coarsely chopped**
 2   **tablespoons chopped fresh cilantro**
 1   **tablespoon chopped dry-roasted peanuts**

1. Stir fish sauce (or soy sauce) and brown sugar in a small bowl. Divide lettuce between 2 plates.

2. Heat 1 teaspoon oil in a medium nonstick skillet over medium-high heat until shimmering but not smoking. Add beef and cook, stirring, until browned on the outside and still pink inside, 1 to 2 minutes. Spoon over the lettuce. Add the remaining 1 teaspoon oil, jalapeño (or serrano), onion and garlic to the pan and cook, stirring, until fragrant, about 1 minute. Add the fish sauce (or soy sauce) mixture, remove from the heat and stir in orange and cilantro. Spoon the sauce over the salads and sprinkle with peanuts.

MAKES **2** SERVINGS.

Quinoa, Mango & Black Bean Salad

The vibrant colors of this salad—orange, red, black and green—signal that it's loaded with phytochemicals, vitamins and minerals. And since it features both quinoa—a "complete" protein with all the essential amino acids—and black beans, it's a vegetarian protein powerhouse. Serve on a bed of Boston lettuce or in a pita pocket.

½ **cup quinoa (*see Note*)**
1 **cup water**
¼ **cup orange juice**
¼ **cup chopped fresh cilantro**
2 **tablespoons rice vinegar**
2 **teaspoons toasted sesame oil**
1 **teaspoon minced fresh ginger**
⅛ **teaspoon salt**
 Pinch of cayenne pepper
1 **small mango, diced (*see Tip, page 244*)**
1 **small red bell pepper, diced**
1 **cup canned black beans (*see Tips for Two, page 248*), rinsed**
2 **scallions, thinly sliced**

1 Toast quinoa in a small dry saucepan over medium heat, stirring often, until it crackles and becomes aromatic, 4 to 6 minutes. Transfer to a fine sieve and rinse thoroughly. Return the quinoa to the pot and add water. Bring to a simmer; reduce heat to maintain a simmer. Cover and cook until the quinoa is tender and the liquid has been absorbed, 15 to 20 minutes.

2 Meanwhile, whisk orange juice, cilantro, vinegar, oil, ginger, salt and cayenne in a medium bowl. Add mango, bell pepper, beans and scallions; toss to coat.

3 When the quinoa is finished cooking, add to the mango mixture and toss to combine.

MAKES 2 SERVINGS.

Active Minutes: **20**

Total: **40 minutes**

To Make Ahead: **Cover and refrigerate for up to 2 days. Serve chilled.**

Per Serving: **422 calories; 9 g fat (1 g sat, 2 g mono); 0 mg cholesterol; 74 g carbohydrate; 15 g protein; 19 g fiber; 256 mg sodium; 642 mg potassium.**

Nutrition Bonus: **Vitamin C (210% daily value), Vitamin A (50% dv), Magnesium (22% dv), Vitamin E (20% dv).**

High ⬆ Fiber

Ingredient Note:

● Quinoa, a delicately flavored grain, was a staple in the ancient Incas' diet. Toasting it before cooking enhances its flavor, and rinsing removes any residue of saponin, quinoa's natural, bitter protective covering.

Greek Salad with Tofu

Tofu boosts the protein in this Greek salad, making it substantial enough for a whole meal. But this dish would also be a perfect addition to a mezze, a Middle Eastern meal of "small dishes"; serve it with warmed whole-wheat pitas, store-bought hummus, stuffed grape leaves, tzatziki (cucumber sauce) and your favorite olives.

Active Minutes: **30**

Total: 30 minutes

Per Serving: 164 calories; 12 g fat (3 g sat, 6 g mono); 13 mg cholesterol; 8 g carbohydrate; 8 g protein; 2 g fiber; 499 mg sodium; 296 mg potassium.

Nutrition Bonus: Vitamin C (35% daily value), Calcium (20% dv).

Healthy)(Weight

Lower ⬇ Carbs

Tip:

- Small amounts of olives can be purchased from bulk bins and salad bars (*see Tips for Two, page 248*).

- 3 tablespoons crumbled feta cheese
- 2 tablespoons chopped red onion *or* scallion
- 6 Kalamata olives (*see Tip*), pitted and chopped
- 1½ tablespoons lemon juice
- 1½ teaspoons extra-virgin olive oil
- ¾ teaspoon dried oregano
- ½ cup drained and crumbled firm tofu
- ⅛ teaspoon salt
- ⅛ teaspoon freshly ground pepper
- 1 small tomato, coarsely chopped
- ½ small cucumber, coarsely chopped
- 1 tablespoon chopped fresh parsley

1. Combine feta, onion (or scallion), olives, lemon juice, oil and oregano in a medium bowl. Add tofu and mash with a fork. Season with salt and pepper. Cover and refrigerate for 10 minutes.

2. Add tomato, cucumber and parsley to the tofu mixture and stir to combine.

MAKES **2** SERVINGS.

Orzo Salad with Chickpeas & Artichoke Hearts

Quintessential Greek flavors—feta, lemon and dill—combine perfectly in this hearty salad. To complete the Mediterranean mood, try pairing it with a Greek Retsina or a Portuguese Vinho Verde.

½	**cup orzo *or* other tiny pasta**
1½	**teaspoons extra-virgin olive oil**
1	**clove garlic, crushed and peeled**
⅛	**teaspoon salt**
1½	**tablespoons lemon juice**
⅛	**teaspoon freshly ground pepper**
1	**14-ounce can artichoke hearts, drained and chopped**
1	**7-ounce can chickpeas, rinsed**
⅓	**cup crumbled feta cheese**
2	**tablespoons chopped fresh dill**
1½	**tablespoons chopped fresh mint**
1	**large tomato, chopped**
2	**cups baby spinach leaves**

Active Minutes: **30**

Total: 30 minutes

To Make Ahead: **Prepare the salad—without the tomatoes and spinach—cover and refrigerate for up to 1 day. Add the tomatoes just before serving and serve over the spinach.**

Per Serving: 431 calories; 8 g fat (2 g sat, 3 g mono); 5 mg cholesterol; 74 g carbohydrate; 18 g protein; 9 g fiber; 705 mg sodium; 527 mg potassium.

Nutrition Bonus: **Vitamin C (50% daily value), Vitamin A (40% dv), Iron (35% dv).**

High ⬆ **Fiber**

1. Bring a small saucepan of water to a boil. Cook orzo until just tender, about 9 minutes, or according to package directions. Drain and rinse under cold water until cool. Press to remove excess water. Transfer to a medium bowl and toss with oil.

2. Mash garlic and salt into a paste with the back of a spoon in a medium bowl. Whisk in lemon juice and pepper. Add the cooked orzo, artichokes, chickpeas, feta, dill and mint; toss gently to combine. Add tomatoes and toss again.

3. Divide spinach between 2 plates and top with the salad.

MAKES **2** SERVINGS.

CHAPTER 2

Soups & Stews

Vegetable Lover's Chicken Soup

C lassic comfort food is yours, in just slightly more than half an hour. Serve with some crusty whole-grain bread or Garlic-Tomato Toasts (*page 229*) and top with grated Romano or Parmesan cheese.

Active Minutes: **35**

Total: **40** minutes

To Make Ahead: Cover and refrigerate up to 3 days or freeze up to 3 months.

Per Serving: 261 calories; 8 g fat (1 g sat, 5 g mono); 72 mg cholesterol; 12 g carbohydrate; 31 g protein; 2 g fiber; 355 mg sodium; 483 mg potassium.

Nutrition Bonus: Vitamin A (70% daily value), Vitamin C (45% dv), Folate (22% dv).

Healthy ⊁ Weight

Lower ⬇ Carbs

1	**tablespoon extra-virgin olive oil**
8	**ounces chicken tenders, cut into bite-size chunks**
1	**small zucchini, finely diced**
1	**large shallot, finely chopped**
½	**teaspoon Italian seasoning blend**
⅛	**teaspoon salt**
2	**plum tomatoes, chopped**
1	**14-ounce can reduced-sodium chicken broth**
¼	**cup dry white wine**
2	**tablespoons orzo *or* other tiny pasta, such as farfelline**
1½	**cups packed baby spinach**

1 Heat oil in a large saucepan over medium-high heat. Add chicken and cook, stirring occasionally, until browned, 3 to 4 minutes. Transfer to a plate.

2 Add zucchini, shallot, Italian seasoning and salt and cook, stirring often, until the vegetables are slightly softened, 2 to 3 minutes. Add tomatoes, broth, wine and orzo (or other tiny pasta); increase heat to high and bring to a boil, stirring occasionally. Reduce heat to a simmer and cook until the pasta is tender, about 8 minutes, or according to package directions. Stir in spinach, the cooked chicken and any accumulated juices from the chicken; cook, stirring, until the chicken is heated through, about 2 minutes.

MAKES **2** SERVINGS, **2** CUPS EACH.

Rustic Mexican Stew

A fiesta-in-a-bowl, this stew gets vibrant colors and flavor from scallions, carrots, jalapeños, tomatoes, cilantro and a whole ear of corn. Top it with diced avocado, hot sauce or salsa.

Active Minutes: **25**

Total: 30 minutes

To Make Ahead: Add all the ingredients except the cilantro. Cover and refrigerate for up to 3 days. Reheat; stir in cilantro before serving.

Per Serving: 277 calories; 14 g fat (3 g sat, 8 g mono); 53 mg cholesterol; 20 g carbohydrate; 20 g protein; 4 g fiber; 464 mg sodium; 561 mg potassium.

Nutrition Bonus: Vitamin A (120% daily value), Vitamin C (40% dv), Potassium (16% dv), Iron (15% dv).

Healthy)(Weight

Lower ⬇ Carbs

- 3 **teaspoons extra-virgin olive oil, divided**
- 2 **boneless, skinless chicken thighs, trimmed of fat**
- 4 **cloves garlic, minced**
- 2 **scallions, sliced, white and green parts divided**
- 1 **carrot, peeled and sliced**
- 1 **jalapeño pepper, seeded and finely chopped**
- ¼ **teaspoon salt**
- ¼ **teaspoon freshly ground pepper**
- 2 **teaspoons ground cumin**
- 1 **14-ounce can reduced-sodium chicken broth**
- 2 **plum tomatoes, diced**
- 1 **ear of corn, husked and cut into 4 pieces**
- 1 **tablespoon lime juice**
- 2 **tablespoons finely chopped fresh cilantro**

1. Heat 2 teaspoons oil in a large saucepan over medium-high heat. Add chicken and cook until browned, about 2 minutes per side. Transfer the chicken to a plate.

2. Add the remaining 1 teaspoon oil, garlic, scallion whites, carrot, jalapeño, salt and pepper to the pot and stir to combine. Cover, reduce heat to medium-low and cook until the vegetables begin to soften, 1 to 2 minutes. Uncover, add cumin and cook, stirring constantly, until fragrant, about 1 minute. Add broth, tomatoes, corn and the cooked chicken; increase heat to medium-high and bring to a simmer, stirring occasionally. Cover, reduce heat to maintain a slow simmer and cook until the vegetables are tender, 5 to 7 minutes. Remove from the heat and stir in scallion greens, lime juice and cilantro.

MAKES **2** SERVINGS, **2** CUPS EACH.

New Mexican Posole

Posole, originally from Jalisco, Mexico, is traditionally served around Christmastime. It's so tasty and—with a few convenience items like canned hominy and chili powder—easy to make that we like it any time of year. Shredded cheese, cilantro or thinly sliced radishes are traditional toppings for this stew.

1	**teaspoon dried oregano**
1/2	**cup chopped red onion, divided**
2	**teaspoons canola oil**
	Pinch of salt
1	**small clove garlic, finely chopped**
1/2-1	**teaspoon chili powder, to taste**
1	**14-ounce can reduced-sodium chicken broth**
1	**15-ounce can hominy (*see Note, page 246*), rinsed**
1	**cup canned black beans *or* pinto beans, rinsed (*see Tips for Two, page 248*)**
6	**ounces boneless, skinless chicken breast, trimmed of fat and cut into 3/4-inch pieces**
1/2	**cup finely shredded green cabbage**
2	**lime wedges**

1. Toast oregano in a small dry skillet over medium-high heat until fragrant, about 30 seconds. Transfer to a plate to cool. Combine 1/2 teaspoon toasted oregano and 2 tablespoons onion in a small bowl.

2. Heat oil in a medium saucepan over medium heat. Add the remaining 6 tablespoons onion and salt; cover and cook over medium heat until the onions are translucent, about 2 minutes. Add garlic and cook for 1 minute. Add the remaining 1/2 teaspoon toasted oregano and chili powder and cook for 1 minute. Add broth and hominy, bring to a simmer and cook for 5 minutes. Add beans and chicken; return to a simmer and cook until the chicken is no longer pink in the middle, about 5 minutes. Top with cabbage and the reserved onion-oregano mixture. Serve with lime wedges.

MAKES **2** SERVINGS, **2** CUPS EACH.

Active Minutes: **25**

Total: 30 minutes

To Make Ahead: Add all ingredients except the reserved oregano-onion mixture, cabbage and lime wedges. Cover and refrigerate for up to 3 days or freeze for up to 3 months. Reheat and garnish before serving.

Per Serving: 358 calories; 8 g fat (1 g sat, 4 g mono); 50 mg cholesterol; 42 g carbohydrate; 28 g protein; 9 g fiber; 541 mg sodium; 298 mg potassium.

Nutrition Bonus: Selenium (27% daily value), Iron & Vitamin C (20% dv).

High ⬆ **Fiber**

Curried Squash & Chicken Soup

Red Thai curry paste adds heat and depth of flavor to this simple soup. If you like, omit the chicken and spinach to make an even simpler first-course soup.

Active Minutes: 15

Total: 20 minutes

Per Serving: 274 calories; 7 g fat (4 g sat, 1 g mono); 63 mg cholesterol; 28 g carbohydrate; 27 g protein; 8 g fiber; 521 mg sodium; 1,288 mg potassium.

Nutrition Bonus: Vitamin A (310% daily value), Vitamin C (70% dv), Folate (49% dv), Potassium (37% dv).

Healthy ⫶ Weight

High ⬆ Fiber

1	**10-ounce package frozen pureed winter squash**
½	**cup "lite" coconut milk (*see Tips for Two, page 248*)**
½	**cup water**
8	**ounces boneless, skinless chicken breast, thinly sliced**
1	**6-ounce bag baby spinach**
2	**teaspoons lime juice**
2	**teaspoons brown sugar**
½-1	**teaspoon Thai red curry paste (*see Note*)**
¼	**teaspoon salt**

Heat squash, coconut milk and water in a medium saucepan over medium-high heat. Cook, stirring occasionally, until the squash defrosts, about 10 minutes. Add chicken, reduce heat to medium and simmer, stirring occasionally, for 3 minutes. Stir in spinach, lime juice, sugar, curry paste to taste and salt and continue cooking until the chicken is cooked through, about 3 minutes longer.

MAKES 2 SERVINGS, 1 3/4 CUPS EACH.

Ingredient Note:

● Red curry paste is a blend of chile peppers, garlic, lemongrass and galanga (a root with a flavor similar to ginger). Look for it in jars or cans in the Asian section of the supermarket or specialty stores.

Lentil & Chicken Stew

Herb and citrus exist in perfect balance in this protein-packed stew flavored with dill and lemon. Serve with slices of whole-grain baguette and a green salad.

Active Minutes: **30**

Total: **40 minutes**

To Make Ahead: Cover and refrigerate for up to 3 days or freeze for up to 3 months.

Per Serving: **369** calories; 11 g fat (2 g sat, 6 g mono); 50 mg cholesterol; 37 g carbohydrate; 33 g protein; 10 g fiber; 520 mg sodium; 1,140 mg potassium.

Nutrition Bonus: **Vitamin A** (260% daily value), Vitamin C (50% dv), Folate (43% dv), Potassium (33% dv).

High ⬆ Fiber

Ingredient Note:

● French green lentils are firmer than brown lentils and cook more quickly. They can be found in natural-foods stores and some large supermarkets.

- **3** teaspoons extra-virgin olive oil, divided
- **8** ounces boneless, skinless chicken breast, diced
- **1** carrot, peeled and finely diced
- **4** cloves garlic, minced
- **1** teaspoon whole coriander seed, crushed (*see Tip, page 244*)
- **⅛** teaspoon salt
- **¼** teaspoon freshly ground pepper
- **1** 14-ounce can reduced-sodium chicken broth
- **½** cup French green *or* brown lentils, sorted and rinsed (*see Note*)
- **1** 6-ounce bag baby spinach
- **1** tablespoon lemon juice
- **1** tablespoon chopped fresh dill

1. Heat 1 teaspoon oil in a large saucepan over medium-high heat. Add chicken and cook, stirring once or twice, until no longer pink in the middle, about 2 minutes. Transfer the chicken to a plate with a slotted spoon.

2. Add the remaining 2 teaspoons oil to the pan and heat over medium-low heat. Add carrot, garlic, coriander, salt and pepper and cook, stirring constantly, until fragrant, 30 seconds to 1 minute. Stir in broth and lentils, increase heat to medium-high and bring to a simmer. Reduce heat to maintain a simmer and cook, stirring occasionally, until the lentils are tender, 20 to 30 minutes (brown lentils take a little longer).

3. Add the cooked chicken, spinach and lemon juice and return to a simmer. Cook until heated through, 1 to 2 minutes. Stir in dill.

MAKES **2** SERVINGS, 1 ¾ CUPS EACH.

Chicken, Parsnip & Apple Stew

Modest, sweet parsnips shine in this autumnal stew. Try pairing it with sandwiches of toasted sharp Cheddar on country wheat and a robust dark beer for a warming fall supper.

3   teaspoons extra-virgin olive oil, divided
1   small onion, finely chopped
2   parsnips, peeled and finely chopped
1   carrot, peeled and finely chopped
1   Granny Smith apple, peeled and finely chopped
1   teaspoon chopped fresh rosemary
¼   teaspoon salt
⅛   teaspoon freshly ground pepper
1   14-ounce can reduced-sodium chicken broth
1   cup water
1   teaspoon cider vinegar
8   ounces chicken tenders, cut into bite-size chunks

1. Heat 2 teaspoons oil in a large saucepan over medium-high heat. Add onion, parsnips, carrot, apple, rosemary, salt and pepper and cook, stirring often, until the vegetables begin to soften, about 8 minutes. Add broth and water and bring to a simmer over high heat. Reduce heat to maintain a simmer and cook, stirring often, until the vegetables are very tender, about 10 minutes.

2. Transfer the soup to a blender; add vinegar, cover and pulse until it forms a chunky puree. (Use caution when pureeing hot liquids; *see Tip, page 244.*)

3. Clean the pot, return it to medium-high heat and add the remaining 1 teaspoon oil. Add chicken and cook, stirring occasionally, until lightly browned, 3 to 4 minutes. Pour the soup back into the pan. Cook, scraping up any browned bits from the bottom of the pan, until heated through, about 1 minute.

MAKES **2** SERVINGS, **2** CUPS EACH.

Active Minutes: **35**

Total: 35 minutes

To Make Ahead: Cover and refrigerate up to 3 days or freeze up to 3 months.

Per Serving: 321 calories; 8 g fat (1 g sat, 6 g mono); 70 mg cholesterol; 34 g carbohydrate; 31 g protein; 7 g fiber; 472 mg sodium; 619 mg potassium.

Nutrition Bonus: Vitamin A (150% daily value), Vitamin C (35% dv), Folate (19% dv), Potassium (18% dv).

High ⬆ Fiber

Spicy Chicken Soup (*Dak Yookgaejang*)

Chicken is substituted for shredded beef for a lighter version of this Korean favorite. The chili powder adds a nice kick, making it a warming winter meal. Serve with individual bowls of rice on the side.

- 4 **cups water**
- 8 **ounces boneless, skinless chicken breast, trimmed of fat**
- 4 **cloves garlic, minced**
- 1 **tablespoon chili powder, preferably Korean (*see Note, page 246*)**
- 2 **teaspoons reduced-sodium soy sauce**
- 1/4 **teaspoon salt, or to taste**
- 1 **large egg**
- 2 **teaspoons toasted sesame oil**
- 4 **scallions, trimmed and cut into 1 1/2-inch pieces**
  Pinch of freshly ground pepper

Active Minutes: **30**

Total: **45 minutes**

To Make Ahead: Cover and refrigerate for up to 1 day.

Per Serving: 237 calories; 10 g fat (2 g sat, 4 g mono); 168 mg cholesterol; 7 g carbohydrate; 28 g protein; 2 g fiber; 661 mg sodium; 430 mg potassium.

Nutrition Bonus: Vitamin A (50% daily value), Selenium (41% dv), Vitamin C (15% dv).

Healthy)(Weight

Lower ⬇ Carbs

1. Place water and chicken in a large saucepan; bring to a boil over high heat. Cover, reduce heat to low and simmer gently, skimming any foam from the surface with a slotted spoon. Cook until the chicken is cooked through and no longer pink in the middle, 10 to 12 minutes. Transfer the chicken to a cutting board, reserving the cooking liquid. When cool enough to handle, use 2 forks to shred the chicken into thin strips.

2. Combine garlic, chili powder, soy sauce, salt and 2 tablespoons of the reserved cooking liquid in a medium bowl. Add the shredded chicken and mix thoroughly. Cover and set aside to marinate for 5 minutes.

3. Whisk egg and oil in a small bowl until well combined.

4. Bring the remaining cooking liquid to a boil over high heat. Add the seasoned chicken mixture, scallions and pepper. Return to a boil; drizzle the egg mixture slowly over the boiling soup. Serve immediately.

MAKES **2** SERVINGS, ABOUT **2** CUPS EACH.

White Chili

Yes, we have no tomatoes... This fragrant "white" chili is a delicious alternative to traditional "red" versions. Serve with lime wedges and a spoonful of light sour cream or a sprinkling of cheese.

2 teaspoons canola oil, divided
1 small onion, chopped
4 ounces ground chicken *or* turkey breast
1 4-ounce can chopped green chiles
¼ teaspoon dried oregano
¼ teaspoon ground cumin
   Pinch to ⅛ teaspoon cayenne pepper, to taste
1 15-ounce can white beans, rinsed
1 cup reduced-sodium chicken broth (*see Tips for Two*)
1 teaspoon cider vinegar *or* 2 teaspoons lime juice

Heat 1 teaspoon oil in a large saucepan over medium heat. Add onion and cook, stirring occasionally, until softened, about 5 minutes. Add the remaining 1 teaspoon oil and chicken (or turkey) and increase heat to medium-high. Cook, using the back of a spoon to break up the meat, until browned, about 2 minutes. Stir in chiles, oregano, cumin and cayenne. Cook, stirring occasionally, until fragrant, about 1 minute. Stir in beans and broth; bring to a simmer. Cook, stirring occasionally, until slightly reduced, about 10 minutes. Add vinegar (or lime juice).

MAKES 2 SERVINGS, 1 ¼ CUPS EACH.

Active Minutes: **30**

Total: 30 minutes

To Make Ahead: Cover and refrigerate for up to 3 days or freeze for up to 3 months.

Per Serving: 273 calories; 10 g fat (2 g sat, 3 g mono); 40 mg cholesterol; 34 g carbohydrate; 21 g protein; 9 g fiber; 554 mg sodium; 558 mg potassium.

Nutrition Bonus: Vitamin C (35% daily value), Folate (19% dv).

High ⬆ Fiber

Tips for Two

CHICKEN BROTH
STORAGE: Leftover canned broth keeps for up to 5 days in the refrigerator or up to 3 months in your freezer. Leftover broths in aseptic packages keep for up to 1 week in the refrigerator. USES: Add to soups, sauces and stews; use for cooking rice and grains; add a little when reheating leftovers to prevent them from drying out.

Creamy Artichoke & Spinach Soup

Pureed artichoke hearts in addition to eggs thicken this delectable version of the classic Greek soup, *avgolemono*. The lemony broth and rice remain as they do in the original. Wilted spinach adds extra color and nutrients.

2	14-ounce cans reduced-sodium chicken broth
1/4	cup long-grain white rice, such as basmati
4	cups packed baby spinach
1	14-ounce can artichoke hearts, rinsed
2	large eggs
2-3	tablespoons lemon juice, to taste
1 1/2	tablespoons chopped fresh dill
1/8	teaspoon freshly ground pepper

Active Minutes: 20

Total: 30 minutes

To Make Ahead: Cover and refrigerate for up to 2 days. Reheat over low heat, without boiling.

Per Serving: 230 calories; 6 g fat (2 g sat, 2 g mono); 218 mg cholesterol; 27 g carbohydrate; 18 g protein; 6 g fiber; 780 mg sodium; 424 mg potassium.

Nutrition Bonus: Vitamin A (130% daily value), Vitamin C (70% dv), Folate (36% dv), Iron (15% dv).

Healthy)(Weight

High ⬆ Fiber

1. Bring broth and rice to a boil in a large saucepan over high heat. Reduce heat to a simmer and cook, uncovered, until the rice is very tender, about 15 minutes. Stir in spinach.

2. Place artichoke hearts, eggs and lemon juice in a blender; cover and puree. With the motor running, ladle about half of the rice mixture into the blender and puree until smooth. (Use caution when pureeing hot liquids; *see Tip, page 244.*) Return the pureed mixture to the pan and cook, stirring constantly, until an instant-read thermometer registers 160°F, reducing the heat as necessary to prevent the soup from boiling. Stir in dill and pepper.

MAKES 2 SERVINGS, 2 1/4 CUPS EACH.

Creamy Fish Chowder

Low-fat milk and mashed potatoes make this chowder so rich and creamy you won't miss the actual cream. Farm-raised tilapia and abundant Pacific cod—both with tender, flaky textures—are ocean-friendly choices.

- **1 slice bacon, diced**
- **1 small onion, chopped**
- **1 stalk celery, chopped**
- **1 clove garlic, minced**
- **1 cup bottled clam juice *or* reduced-sodium chicken broth (*see Tips for Two, page 248*)**
- **8 ounces tilapia *or* Pacific cod fillets, cut into 1-inch cubes**
- **2 small russet potatoes, peeled and diced (about 2 cups)**
- **1 teaspoon chopped fresh thyme *or* ¼ teaspoon dried**
- **1 bay leaf**
- **2/3 cup low-fat milk**
- **1 tablespoon water**
- **2 teaspoons cornstarch**
- **1/8 teaspoon freshly ground pepper**
- **2 teaspoons chopped fresh parsley (optional)**

Active Minutes: **30**

Total: 40 minutes

Per Serving: 323 calories; 5 g fat (2 g sat, 1 g mono); 67 mg cholesterol; 40 g carbohydrate; 31 g protein; 3 g fiber; 759 mg sodium; 1121 mg potassium.

Nutrition Bonus: Vitamin C (60% daily value), Potassium (32% dv), Magnesium (19% dv), Folate (16% dv).

1. Heat a large saucepan over medium heat. Add bacon and cook, stirring often, until crisp, 3 to 5 minutes. Transfer the bacon with a slotted spoon to a paper towel-lined plate to drain.

2. Add onion, celery and garlic to the bacon drippings and cook, stirring occasionally, until softened, 3 to 5 minutes. Add clam juice (or chicken broth), fish, potatoes, thyme and bay leaf and bring to a simmer. Cover, reduce heat to maintain a simmer, and cook until the potatoes are tender, 10 to 12 minutes. Discard the bay leaf. With a slotted spoon, transfer about 2/3 cup of the solids to a bowl and mash with a potato masher or fork. Return to the pot and add the milk. Bring to a simmer.

3. Whisk water and cornstarch in a small bowl. When the soup comes to a simmer, gradually add the cornstarch mixture. Cook, stirring constantly, until thickened, about 1 minute. Season with pepper. Serve garnished with the cooked bacon and parsley, if using.

MAKES **2** SERVINGS, 1 3/4 CUPS EACH.

Spicy Cioppino

San Francisco's Italian immigrants developed this stew to use the abundant local seafood. We've opted for farm-raised tilapia and scallops, but feel free to experiment with whatever is fresh.

- **4 small (1- to 2-inch-diameter) red potatoes, quartered**
- **2 tablespoons extra-virgin olive oil, divided**
- **1 tilapia fillet, diced (about 5 ounces)**
- **4 ounces dry bay scallops (*see Note, page 247*), patted dry**
- **1 small sweet onion, sliced**
- **2 teaspoons Italian seasoning blend *or* poultry seasoning**
- **1-2 teaspoons hot paprika**
- **¼ teaspoon salt**
- **¼ teaspoon freshly ground pepper**
- **1 cup dry white wine**
- **½ cup water**
- **3 plum tomatoes, diced**
- **2 tablespoons capers, rinsed (optional)**
- **2 tablespoons minced fresh parsley (optional)**

Active Minutes: **30**

Total: 30 minutes

Per Serving: 431 calories; 17 g fat (2 g sat, 11 g mono); 56 mg cholesterol; 22 g carbohydrate; 27 g protein; 3 g fiber; 502 mg sodium; 1,041 mg potassium.

Nutrition Bonus: Vitamin C (45% daily value), Potassium & Vitamin A (30% dv), Magnesium (23% dv).

Lower ⬇ Carbs

1. Place potatoes in a saucepan, cover with water and bring to a boil over high heat. Reduce heat and simmer until tender, 10 to 12 minutes. Drain.

2. Meanwhile, heat 1 tablespoon oil in a large saucepan over medium-high heat. Add tilapia and scallops; cook, stirring once or twice, until just opaque, about 2 minutes. Transfer to a plate and cover with foil to keep warm.

3. Add the remaining 1 tablespoon oil and onion to the pan and stir to coat. Cover, reduce heat to medium-low and cook, stirring often, until lightly browned, 5 to 7 minutes. Uncover, increase heat to medium-high, add Italian (or poultry) seasoning, paprika to taste, salt and pepper; cook, stirring, until fragrant, about 30 seconds. Add wine, water and tomatoes; bring to a simmer. Reduce heat to maintain a simmer and cook, stirring often, until the onion is tender, 6 to 8 minutes. Add the fish, scallops, potatoes and capers (if using), return to a simmer and cook until heated through, about 2 minutes. Garnish with parsley, if desired.

MAKES 2 SERVINGS, 2 CUPS EACH.

Corn & Bacon Chowder

Comforting and wholesome, corn chowder served with a green salad makes a satisfying light supper. Stir in some cooked diced or shredded chicken if you crave more protein.

Active Minutes: **40**

Total: 40 minutes

To Make Ahead: Cover and refrigerate for up to 3 days.

Per Serving: 338 calories; 17 g fat (5 g sat, 9 g mono); 15 mg cholesterol; 39 g carbohydrate; 12 g protein; 4 g fiber; 443 mg sodium; 507 mg potassium.

Nutrition Bonus: Vitamin C (25% daily value).

2 **slices bacon, chopped**
1 **tablespoon extra-virgin olive oil**
1 **small onion, finely chopped**
4 **cloves garlic, minced**
½ **teaspoon dried thyme**
⅛ **teaspoon salt**
⅛ **teaspoon freshly ground pepper**
1 **tablespoon all-purpose flour**
1 **14-ounce can reduced-sodium chicken broth**
½ **cup low-fat milk**
1 **cup fresh *or* frozen corn kernels**
1 **cup frozen diced hash brown potatoes**
2 **tablespoons chopped fresh chives**
1 **teaspoon lemon juice *or* rice vinegar**

1 ♦ Heat a medium saucepan over medium heat. Add bacon, and cook, stirring often, until crisp, 3 to 5 minutes. Transfer the bacon with a slotted spoon to a paper towel-lined plate to drain.

2 ♦ Add oil, onion, garlic, thyme, salt and pepper to the pot and stir to combine. Cover and cook, stirring occasionally, until the onion begins to brown and soften, about 3 minutes. Sprinkle flour over the onion mixture and stir to coat. Add broth and milk and bring to a simmer, whisking constantly. Add corn and potatoes, increase heat to medium-high and return to a simmer. Reduce heat to maintain a simmer and cook, stirring often, until the potatoes are tender, 4 to 5 minutes.

3 ♦ Transfer 1 cup of the soup to a blender and puree until smooth. (Use caution when pureeing hot liquids; *see Tip, page 244.*) Return the pureed soup to the saucepan along with chives, lemon juice (or vinegar) and the cooked bacon.

MAKES **2** SERVINGS, **1** ½ CUPS EACH.

Spicy Potato & Kale Soup

Spicy sausage—in this case, chorizo—pairs beautifully with hearty greens. If you like, substitute collard or mustard greens for the kale. If you can't get chorizo, hot Italian sausage will also work in this soup.

- ¼ **cup halved and sliced chorizo sausage (*see Note, page 245*)**
- 1 **teaspoon extra-virgin olive oil**
- 1 **small onion, chopped**
- 1 **14-ounce can reduced-sodium chicken broth**
- ⅓ **cup water**
- 1 **small russet potato, peeled and sliced**
- 2 **cloves garlic, peeled and halved**
- 4 **cups kale, ribs removed, thinly sliced (*see Tips for Two*)**
- ⅛ **teaspoon freshly ground pepper, or to taste**

1 ◆ Heat a large saucepan over medium heat. Add chorizo and cook, stirring, until browned, about 2 minutes. Transfer the chorizo to a paper towel-lined plate; wipe out the pot.

2 ◆ Heat oil in the pot over medium heat. Add onion and cook, stirring occasionally, until softened, about 2 minutes. Add broth, water, potato and garlic; increase the heat to high and bring to a boil. Reduce to a simmer, cover and cook, stirring occasionally, until the potato is tender, 6 to 9 minutes. Lightly mash the potato with a wooden spoon. Add kale, a handful at a time, waiting until it has wilted before adding more. Adjust heat to maintain a simmer and cook, stirring occasionally, until the kale is tender, about 5 minutes. Add the reserved chorizo and season with pepper.

MAKES 2 SERVINGS, 1½ CUPS EACH.

Active Minutes: **30**

Total: **30 minutes**

To Make Ahead: **Cover and refrigerate for up to 3 days or freeze for up to 3 months.**

Per Serving: **206 calories; 9 g fat (3 g sat, 4 g mono); 16 mg cholesterol; 24 g carbohydrate; 11 g protein; 4 g fiber; 306 mg sodium; 676 mg potassium.**

Nutrition Bonus: **Vitamin A (380% daily value), Vitamin C (120% dv), Potassium (19% dv).**

Healthy Ⅹ Weight

Tips for Two

KALE

STORAGE: Refrigerate, preferably in a perforated plastic bag, for 5 to 10 days. USES: Substitute kale in Sautéed Swiss Chard with Chile & Garlic (*page 232*); add during the last 4 minutes while cooking pasta; sauté with minced garlic and extra-virgin olive oil for an omelet filling or to stir into scrambled eggs.

Roasted Tomato & Lentil Soup

Ham lends a subtle, smoky flavor to this robust soup. If you can, purchase "fire-roasted" diced canned tomatoes, they will enhance the smoky notes. Serve with toasted whole-wheat country bread with melted Gruyère on top.

Active Minutes: 15

Total: 40 minutes

To Make Ahead: Cover and refrigerate for up to 3 days or freeze for up to 3 months.

Per Serving: 262 calories; 8 g fat (2 g sat, 4 g mono); 19 mg cholesterol; 33 g carbohydrate; 15 g protein; 7 g fiber; 653 mg sodium; 510 mg potassium.

Nutrition Bonus: Vitamin A (120% daily value), Vitamin C (60% dv), Iron (15% dv).

Healthy ⧓ Weight

High ⬆ Fiber

2   teaspoons extra-virgin olive oil
1   small onion, diced
2   cloves garlic, minced
1   14-ounce can reduced-sodium chicken broth
1   stalk celery, diced
1   carrot, peeled and diced
¼   cup French green lentils (*see Note, page 246*), sorted and rinsed
1   teaspoon Italian seasoning blend
    Pinch of crushed red pepper
1   15-ounce can diced tomatoes, preferably fire-roasted
½   cup shredded cabbage
¼   cup finely diced ham
⅛   teaspoon freshly ground pepper

1. Heat oil in a medium saucepan over medium heat; add onion and garlic and cook, stirring often, until softened, about 3 minutes. Add broth, celery, carrot, lentils, Italian seasoning and crushed red pepper. Bring to a boil over high heat; reduce to a simmer, and cook, covered, until the lentils are almost tender, about 20 minutes. Add tomatoes and their juice, cabbage and ham, return to a simmer and cook until the cabbage is tender, about 10 minutes. Season with pepper.

MAKES 2 SERVINGS, 2 CUPS EACH.

Tunisian Vegetable Tagine

Fragrant vegetable stews are common around the Mediterranean. This streamlined version is flavored with a North African spice blend and simplified with the use of precut, frozen bell peppers and onions.

1	teaspoon extra-virgin olive oil
1½	cups frozen bell pepper and onion mix
½	teaspoon coriander seeds
¼	teaspoon caraway seeds
	Pinch of salt
⅛	teaspoon paprika, plus more for sprinkling
⅛	teaspoon cayenne pepper
2	cloves garlic, minced
1	14-ounce can diced tomatoes
1	8-ounce can chickpeas, rinsed
	Freshly ground pepper to taste
2	large eggs

Active Minutes: **15**

Total: **25 minutes**

To Make Ahead: **Prepare through Step 3. Cover and refrigerate for up to 2 days.**

Per Serving: 259 calories; 9 g fat (2 g sat, 4 g mono); 212 mg cholesterol; 43 g carbohydrate; 13 g protein; 7 g fiber; 564 mg sodium; 231 mg potassium.

Nutrition Bonus: Vitamin A (58% daily value), Vitamin C (53% dv), Selenium (27% dv), Folate (19% dv), Iron (17% dv).

High ⬆ Fiber

1. Heat oil in a large nonstick skillet over medium-high heat. Add pepper and onion mix; cook, stirring occasionally, until most of the liquid has evaporated, 3 to 5 minutes.

2. Meanwhile, coarsely grind coriander seeds, caraway seeds and salt in a spice grinder, dry blender or mortar and pestle. Transfer to a small bowl and stir in paprika and cayenne.

3. Add garlic and the spice mixture to the skillet; cook, stirring, for 30 seconds. Add tomatoes and chickpeas; bring to a simmer. Reduce heat to medium and cook at a lively simmer until slightly thickened, 8 to 12 minutes. Season with pepper.

4. Break eggs into separate halves of the pan, taking care not to break the yolks. Reduce heat to medium-low, cover and cook until the eggs are set, 5 to 7 minutes. Sprinkle the eggs with paprika.

MAKES 2 SERVINGS, 2 CUPS STEW PLUS 1 EGG EACH.

CHAPTER 3

Vegetarian

No-Bake Macaroni & Cheese

Not only is this ultra-creamy version of mac & cheese nearly as fast as the boxed variety, but you will be able to pronounce every ingredient. If you're not a broccoli fan, substitute any frozen vegetable that you or your dining mate desire.

Active Minutes: **20**

Total: **25 minutes**

Per Serving: 451 calories; 15 g fat (9 g sat, 1 g mono); 44 mg cholesterol; 58 g carbohydrate; 24 g protein; 7 g fiber; 660 mg sodium; 251 mg potassium.

Nutrition Bonus: Vitamin C (70% daily value), Calcium (45% dv), Vitamin A (30% dv), Fiber (28% dv).

High ⬆ Fiber

- **4** ounces whole-wheat elbow noodles (1 cup)
- **1** cup frozen chopped broccoli
- **1** cup low-fat milk, divided
- **2** tablespoons all-purpose flour
- **1/4** teaspoon garlic powder
- **1/4** teaspoon salt
- **1/8** teaspoon ground white pepper
- **1/2** cup shredded extra-sharp Cheddar cheese
- **2** tablespoons shredded Parmesan cheese
- **1/2** teaspoon Dijon mustard

1. Bring a large saucepan of water to a boil. Cook noodles for 4 minutes. Add frozen broccoli and continue cooking, stirring occasionally, until the pasta and broccoli are just tender, 4 to 5 minutes more.

2. Meanwhile, heat ¾ cup milk in another large saucepan over medium-high heat until just simmering. Whisk the remaining ¼ cup milk, flour, garlic powder, salt and pepper in a small bowl until combined. Add the flour mixture to the simmering milk. Return to a simmer and cook, whisking constantly, until the mixture is thickened, 2 to 3 minutes. Remove from the heat and whisk in Cheddar, Parmesan and mustard until the cheeses are melted.

3. Drain the pasta and broccoli and add to the cheese sauce. Return to the heat and cook, stirring, over medium-low, until heated through, about 1 minute.

MAKES **2** SERVINGS, 1 1/2 CUPS EACH.

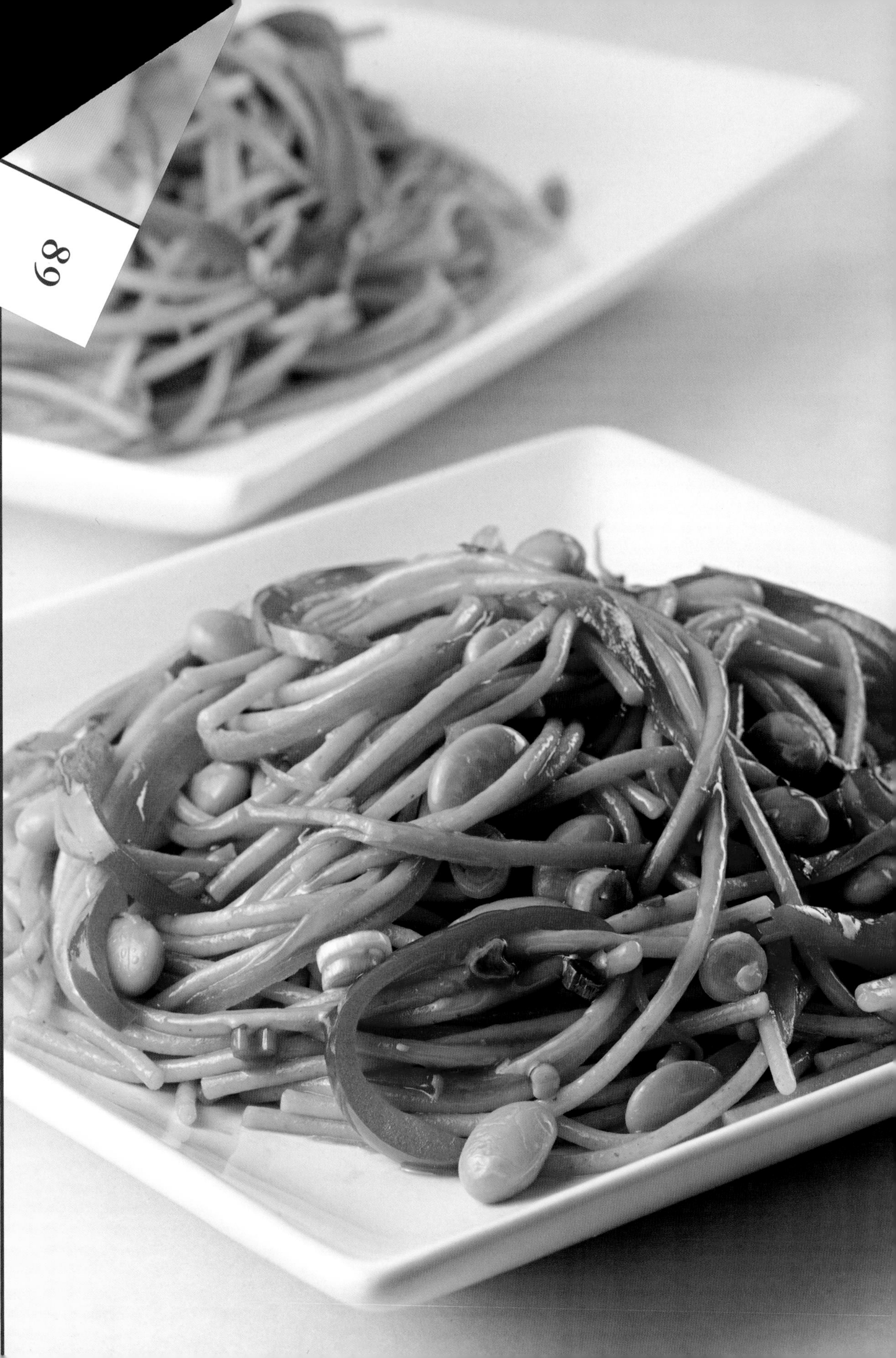

Edamame Lo Mein

As tasty as your favorite Chinese take-out, but far less greasy and salty, this version of lo mein delivers great taste and plenty of protein with the addition of edamame (shelled soybeans), now available—at least in frozen form and often fresh—in almost every supermarket.

4	ounces whole-wheat spaghetti
1	cup frozen edamame (shelled soybeans)
2	scallions, thinly sliced
1½	tablespoons reduced-sodium soy sauce
1	tablespoon rice vinegar
1	tablespoon oyster-flavored sauce *or* oyster sauce (*see Note*)
1	teaspoon sugar
1	teaspoon toasted sesame oil
	Pinch of crushed red pepper
1	tablespoon canola oil
1	medium carrot, peeled and cut into matchsticks
1	small red bell pepper, cut into matchsticks

1. Bring a large saucepan of water to a boil. Add spaghetti and edamame and cook, stirring occasionally, until the pasta is just tender, 8 to 10 minutes or according to package directions. Drain.

2. Meanwhile, whisk scallions, soy sauce, vinegar, oyster sauce, sugar, sesame oil and crushed red pepper in a small bowl until the sugar is dissolved.

3. Heat canola oil in a large nonstick skillet over medium-high heat. Add carrots and bell pepper and cook, stirring often, until slightly softened, 3 to 5 minutes. Add the pasta and edamame. Cook, stirring occasionally, until the pasta is crispy in spots, 1 to 3 minutes. Add the sauce and stir to combine.

MAKES 2 SERVINGS, 2 CUPS EACH.

Active Minutes: **30**

Total: **40 minutes**

Per Serving: 421 calories; 13 g fat (1 g sat, 5 g mono); 0 mg cholesterol; 61 g carbohydrate; 18 g protein; 13 g fiber; 603 mg sodium; 309 mg potassium.

Nutrition Bonus: Vitamin A (140% daily value), Vitamin C (130% dv), Selenium (57% dv), Iron (22% dv).

High ⬆ Fiber

Ingredient Note:

- Oyster sauce is a richly flavored condiment made from oysters and brine; it is often used in Asian cooking. Vegetarian oyster sauces substitute mushrooms for the oysters and can be found at Asian specialty markets or online at asianfoodgrocer.com.

Pomodoro Pasta with White Beans & Olives

Capture the flavor of vine-ripened tomatoes with this elegant-yet-quick fresh tomato sauce. Although it's an uncooked sauce, the beans are heated briefly in the olive oil and garlic to infuse them with flavor.

Active Minutes: **25**

Total: 30 minutes

Per Serving: 481 calories; 16 g fat (3 g sat, 6 g mono); 4 mg cholesterol; 75 g carbohydrate; 21 g protein; 14 g fiber; 906 mg sodium; 816 mg potassium.

Nutrition Bonus: Vitamin C (50% daily value), Iron (25% dv), Potassium (23% dv), Vitamin A (20% dv).

High ⬆ Fiber

Tips for Two
OLIVES
Small amounts of olives can be purchased from bulk bins and salad bars.

- **4**   **ounces whole-wheat pasta shells, tubetti, ziti *or* rigatoni**
- **1**   **tablespoon extra-virgin olive oil**
- **1**   **15-ounce can cannellini beans, rinsed**
- **1**   **large clove garlic, minced**
- **2**   **ripe medium tomatoes, diced**
- **2**   **tablespoons oil-cured black olives (*see Tips for Two*), pitted and chopped**
- **¼**   **cup sliced fresh basil**
-     **Freshly ground pepper to taste**
- **2**   **tablespoons freshly grated Pecorino Romano cheese**

1 Bring a large saucepan of water to a boil. Add pasta and cook, stirring occasionally, until just tender, 8 to 10 minutes or according to package directions. Drain.

2 Meanwhile, heat oil in a large skillet over medium heat. Add beans and garlic and cook, stirring frequently, until the beans are just heated through, 2 to 3 minutes. Remove from the heat. Add tomatoes, olives, basil and pepper. Stir gently to combine. Divide the pasta between 2 plates and top with the bean mixture and cheese.

MAKES **2** SERVINGS, **2** CUPS EACH.

Corn & Tomato Pizzas

Remember English-muffin pizzas? This healthier, grown-up approach uses whole-grain pitas and a variety of vegetables for an almost-instant entree you'll love just as much.

Active Minutes: **15**

Total: 25 minutes

Per Serving: 412 calories; 13 g fat (4 g sat, 5 g mono); 18 mg cholesterol; 56 g carbohydrate; 18 g protein; 9 g fiber; 752 mg sodium; 247 mg potassium.

Nutrition Bonus: Calcium (25% daily value), Vitamin A & Vitamin C (15% dv).

High ↑ Fiber

- 2 **teaspoons extra-virgin olive oil**
- 1 **tablespoon chopped garlic**
- 2 **plum tomatoes, diced**
- ¼ **cup frozen *or* fresh corn kernels**
- 1 **teaspoon red-wine vinegar**
  Pinch of salt
  Pinch of freshly ground pepper
- 2 **6-inch whole-wheat pita breads**
- 4 **oil-cured black olives (*see Tips for Two, page 248*), pitted and chopped**
- ½ **cup shredded mozzarella cheese**
- 2 **tablespoons chopped fresh basil**

1. Position rack in bottom of the oven; preheat to 450°F.

2. Heat oil in a medium skillet over medium-high heat. Add garlic and cook, stirring, until fragrant and beginning to turn golden, 30 seconds to 1 minute. Add tomatoes, corn, vinegar, salt and pepper; cook, stirring often, until heated through, 2 to 3 minutes.

3. Place pitas on a baking sheet. Bake until starting to crisp, about 5 minutes. Top with the tomato mixture, olives and cheese. Bake until the cheese melts, about 5 minutes. Sprinkle with basil, cut into wedges and serve.

MAKES **2** SERVINGS.

Caramelized Onion & Green Olive Pizzas

A flavorful combination of caramelized onions, green olives and feta makes an elegant topping for single-serving pizzas. Accompany these with a salad of romaine, thinly sliced red onions and juicy orange segments, dressed with red-wine vinegar and olive oil.

5	teaspoons extra-virgin olive oil
1	medium onion, sliced
1	teaspoon chopped fresh thyme or 1/4 teaspoon dried
1/4	teaspoon freshly ground pepper
1/4	teaspoon sugar
6	green olives (*see Tips for Two, page 248*), pitted and chopped
2	6-inch whole-wheat pita breads
2	tablespoons crumbled feta cheese, or more to taste

Active Minutes: **20**

Total: **30 minutes**

Per Serving: **433** calories; 19 g fat (3 g sat, 12 g mono); 8 mg cholesterol; 56 g carbohydrate; 12 g protein; 10 g fiber; 797 mg sodium; 128 mg potassium.

High ⬆ Fiber

1. Position rack in bottom third of oven; preheat to 425°F.

2. Heat oil in a large nonstick skillet over medium-high heat. Add onion, thyme, pepper and sugar. Reduce heat to medium-low and cook, stirring often, until the onion is very soft, about 8 minutes. Add olives and remove from the heat.

3. Place pitas on a baking sheet. Divide the onion mixture between the pitas and spread to the edges; sprinkle with feta. Bake until the cheese is golden, about 10 minutes. Cut into wedges and serve.

MAKES **2** SERVINGS.

Pineapple Tofu Stir-Fry

At last—a sweet-and-sour dish with a fresh, not cloying, taste. Add a pinch of crushed red pepper, a splash of chile-garlic sauce or a dash of hot sauce to give it a little heat.

1 **8-ounce can pineapple chunks *or* tidbits, 3 tablespoons juice reserved**
5 **teaspoons rice vinegar**
1 **tablespoon reduced-sodium soy sauce**
1 **tablespoon ketchup**
2 **teaspoons brown sugar**
7 **ounces extra-firm, water-packed tofu (*see Tips for Two, page 248*), drained, rinsed and cut into 1/2-inch cubes**
1 **teaspoon cornstarch**
3 **teaspoons canola oil, divided**
1 **tablespoon minced garlic**
2 **teaspoons minced ginger**
1 **large bell pepper, cut into 1/2-by-2-inch strips**

1. Whisk the reserved 3 tablespoons pineapple juice, vinegar, soy sauce, ketchup and sugar in a small bowl until smooth. Place tofu in a medium bowl; toss with 2 tablespoons of the sauce. Let marinate for 5 minutes. Add cornstarch to the remaining sauce and whisk until smooth.

2. Heat 2 teaspoons oil in a large nonstick skillet over medium-high heat. Transfer the tofu to the skillet using a slotted spoon. Whisk any remaining marinade into the bowl of sauce. Cook the tofu, stirring every 1 to 2 minutes, until golden brown, 7 to 9 minutes total. Transfer the tofu to a plate.

3. Add the remaining 1 teaspoon oil to the skillet and heat over medium heat. Add garlic and ginger and cook, stirring constantly, until fragrant, about 30 seconds. Add bell pepper and cook, stirring often, until just tender, 2 to 3 minutes. Pour in the sauce and cook, stirring, until thickened, about 30 seconds. Add the tofu and pineapple chunks (or tidbits) and cook, stirring gently, until heated through, about 2 minutes more.

MAKES **2** SERVINGS, **1** 1/2 CUPS EACH.

Active Minutes: **35**

Total: **35 minutes**

To Make Ahead: The tofu can marinate (Step 1) for up to 30 minutes.

Per Serving: 263 calories; 12 g fat (1 g sat, 5 g mono); 0 mg cholesterol; 34 g carbohydrate; 10 g protein; 4 g fiber; 368 mg sodium; 549 mg potassium.

Nutrition Bonus: Vitamin C (280% daily value), Vitamin A (50% dv), Calcium (25% dv), Magnesium (18% dv).

Crispy Seitan Stir-Fry

S eitan skeptics, gather 'round! We've found it a terrific ingredient when prepared over high heat, with a bit of oil and a flavorful sauce. Here at EATINGWELL, the skeptics wolfed this down.

Active Minutes: **30**

Total: 30 minutes

Per Serving: 350 calories; 14 g fat (1 g sat, 8 g mono); 0 mg cholesterol; 33 g carbohydrate; 20 g protein; 12 g fiber; 702 mg sodium; 430 mg potassium.

Nutrition Bonus: Vitamin A (240% daily value), Vitamin C (200% dv), Vitamin E (17% dv).

Healthy)(Weight

High ⬆ Fiber

Ingredient Note:

- Seitan, a high-protein product made from wheat gluten, has a meaty texture and is found in health-food stores or large super-markets near the tofu. The package weight varies, depending on whether water weight is included. Look for the "drained weight" on the label.

¼ **cup sherry (see Note, page 247)**
¼ **cup water**
1 **tablespoon hoisin sauce**
1 **teaspoon cornstarch**
1 **tablespoon brown sugar**
1 **tablespoon lime juice**
⅛ **teaspoon salt**
4 **teaspoons canola oil, divided**
8 **ounces water-packed seitan (see Note), preferably chicken-style, drained and patted dry**
2 **tablespoons chopped peanuts**
1 **teaspoon chopped fresh ginger**
2 **carrots, peeled and thinly sliced**
1 **bell pepper, thinly sliced**
2 **tablespoons chopped fresh cilantro (optional)**

1 ◆ Whisk sherry, water, hoisin, cornstarch, brown sugar, lime and salt in a small bowl.

2 ◆ Heat 3 teaspoons oil in a large nonstick skillet over medium-high heat. Add seitan and cook, stirring occasionally, until crispy, 4 to 7 minutes. Add the remaining 1 teaspoon oil, peanuts and ginger and cook, stirring often, until fragrant, about 1 minute. Add carrots and bell pepper; cook, stirring, about 1 minute.

3 ◆ Whisk the sauce again; add it to the pan and stir to coat. Reduce heat to medium, cover and cook until the vegetables are tender-crisp and the sauce is thickened, about 3 minutes. Stir in cilantro, if using.

MAKES **2** SERVINGS, **1** ½ CUPS EACH.

CHAPTER 4

Chicken, Duck & Turkey

Stewed Chicken Thighs with Dried Fruits

Moist, meaty chicken simmers in a rich, mahogany-colored sauce. Dried prunes and apricots work in counterpoint to the touch of vinegar to create an unforgettable savory flavor. You'll want quick-cooking barley or whole-wheat couscous (*see page 239*) to soak it up.

Active Minutes: **20**

Total: 30 minutes

Per Serving: 448 calories; 12 g fat (3 g sat, 6 g mono); 61 mg cholesterol; 67 g carbohydrate; 22 g protein; 9 g fiber; 291 mg sodium; 1,193 mg potassium.

Nutrition Bonus: Vitamin A (60% daily value), Potassium (34% dv), Vitamin C (15% dv).

High ⬆ Fiber

2	teaspoons extra-virgin olive oil
2	bone-in chicken thighs, skin removed
1	small onion, sliced
2	cloves garlic, finely chopped
1	14-ounce can reduced-sodium chicken broth
12	dried apricots, quartered
12	pitted prunes, quartered
2	tablespoons sherry vinegar *or* red-wine vinegar
1/8	teaspoon salt
	Freshly ground pepper to taste
2	tablespoons chopped fresh parsley

1. Heat oil in a large saucepan over medium-high heat. Add chicken thighs and cook until golden, about 2 minutes per side. Add onion and garlic and cook, stirring occasionally, until softened, 2 to 3 minutes. Add broth, apricots, prunes and vinegar. Bring to a boil; reduce heat to low. Cover and simmer until the chicken is no longer pink in the middle, about 6 minutes. Transfer the chicken to a plate and cover with foil to keep warm.

2. Increase heat to high and bring the sauce to a boil. Boil until slightly thickened, about 5 minutes. Season with salt and pepper. Serve the chicken topped with the sauce and garnished with parsley.

MAKES **2** SERVINGS.

Jimmo's Chicken & Okra

Comfort food with a Southern accent, this dish was inspired by our friend, Jimmo, who ate it growing up in South Carolina. Serve over brown rice or Quick Cheese Grits (*page 228*).

- **1 tablespoon extra-virgin olive oil**
- **1 medium onion, chopped**
- **½ cup frozen corn kernels**
- **8 ounces boneless, skinless chicken thighs, trimmed of fat and cut into 1-inch chunks**
- **2 cloves garlic, minced**
- **1 teaspoon paprika**
- **Pinch of cayenne pepper, or to taste**
- **1 14-ounce can diced tomatoes, preferably fire-roasted**
- **1 cup frozen chopped okra**
- **¼ teaspoon freshly ground pepper**
- **⅛ teaspoon salt**

Heat oil in a large nonstick skillet over medium-high heat. Add onion and corn and cook, stirring often, until lightly browned and softened, about 4 minutes. Add chicken and cook, stirring often, until browned, about 2 minutes. Add garlic, paprika and cayenne and cook, stirring, until fragrant, about 30 seconds. Add tomatoes and okra. Bring to a boil, reduce heat to a simmer. Cover and cook, stirring occasionally, until the chicken is cooked through, about 5 minutes. Add pepper and salt.

MAKES **2** SERVINGS, **1** ½ CUPS EACH.

Active Minutes: **30**

Total: **30 minutes**

Per Serving: 369 calories; 16 g fat (3 g sat, 9 g mono); 76 mg cholesterol; 31 g carbohydrate; 27 g protein; 7 g fiber; 658 mg sodium; 620 mg potassium.

Nutrition Bonus: Vitamin C (70% daily value), Folate (39% dv), Vitamin A (35% dv), Iron & Zinc (20% dv), Calcium (15% dv).

High ⬆ Fiber

Chicken Cassoulet

A classic cassoulet takes two days to make and is larded with fat. This version keeps it simple with one skillet and a "lite" touch. Serve with some crusty whole-grain rolls.

Active Minutes: **35**

Total: **40 minutes**

To Make Ahead: Cover and refrigerate for up to 3 days.

Per Serving: 411 calories; 14 g fat (3 g sat, 6 g mono); 76 mg cholesterol; 43 g carbohydrate; 32 g protein; 11 g fiber; 854 mg sodium; 667 mg potassium.

Nutrition Bonus: Iron & Zinc (20% daily value), Potassium (19% dv), Calcium (15% dv).

High ↑ Fiber

Toasted Breadcrumbs:

● Toss 1/4 cup whole-wheat breadcrumbs with 1 teaspoon extra-virgin olive oil. Toast the breadcrumbs in a large skillet over medium-high heat, stirring often, until they are golden and crisp, 1 to 2 minutes.

1	15-ounce can white beans, rinsed
1	teaspoon extra-virgin olive oil
6	ounces boneless, skinless chicken thighs, trimmed of fat and cut into 1 1/2-inch chunks
1	small onion, chopped
2	cloves garlic, roughly chopped
1	tablespoon plus 1/4 cup water, divided
1/4	teaspoon dried rosemary
1/4	teaspoon dried thyme
1/4	teaspoon freshly ground pepper
1/4	cup dry white wine
1/4	cup reduced-sodium chicken broth (*see Tips for Two, page 248*)
3	ounces low-fat turkey kielbasa, sliced into 1/2-inch pieces
1/4	cup Toasted Breadcrumbs (*see Note*)

1. Place 1/4 cup beans in a small bowl and mash roughly with a fork or potato masher. Add the remaining beans to the bowl.

2. Heat oil in a large skillet over medium heat. Add chicken in a single layer. Cook, turning once, until browned on both sides, 2 to 3 minutes per side. Transfer to a plate and cover with foil to keep warm.

3. Add onion and garlic to the pan. Cook, stirring, until fragrant, about 1 minute. Add 1 tablespoon water. Cover and cook, stirring occasionally, until the onion is softened and browned, about 4 minutes. Add rosemary, thyme and pepper. Cook, stirring, until fragrant, about 30 seconds. Add wine; increase heat to high. Cook, stirring with a wooden spoon to scrape up any browned bits, until the wine has reduced by about half, 30 seconds to 1 minute. Add the remaining 1/4 cup water, broth, kielbasa, the beans and chicken; bring to a boil. Reduce heat to a simmer, cover and cook until the chicken is cooked through, 3 to 5 minutes. Serve topped with Toasted Breadcrumbs.

MAKES **2** SERVINGS.

Chicken Forestière

A *la forestière* ("of the forest") is characterized by deep, hearty flavors, usually including mushrooms. Our version is lighter than the French classic but still has every bit of the flavor.

- **3 tablespoons all-purpose flour, divided**
- **¼ teaspoon salt**
- **¼ teaspoon freshly ground pepper**
- **2 boneless, skinless chicken breasts, trimmed of fat (8 ounces)**
- **3 teaspoons canola oil, divided**
- **2 tablespoons minced shallot *or* onion**
- **2 cups sliced mushrooms**
- **¾ cup reduced-sodium chicken broth (*see Tips for Two*)**
- **½ cup dry white wine**
- **1 tablespoon chopped fresh parsley *or* chives**

1. Combine 2 tablespoons flour, salt and pepper in a shallow dish. Dredge chicken in the flour mixture.

2. Heat 2 teaspoons oil in a large nonstick skillet over medium heat. Add the chicken and cook until golden and cooked through, 3 to 4 minutes per side, adjusting heat as necessary to prevent burning. Transfer to a plate and cover with foil to keep warm.

3. Increase the heat to medium-high and add the remaining 1 teaspoon oil to the pan. Add shallot (or onion) and cook, stirring, until fragrant, about 15 seconds. Add mushrooms and cook, stirring occasionally, until softened and browned, 1 to 2 minutes. Sprinkle the mushrooms with the remaining 1 tablespoon flour and cook, stirring, for 30 seconds. Pour in broth and wine and bring to a boil, stirring constantly. Reduce heat to a steady simmer and cook, stirring occasionally, until slightly thickened, about 5 minutes.

4. Reduce heat to low and stir in parsley (or chives). Return the chicken to the pan, turn to coat with the sauce, and cook until heated through, 3 to 5 minutes.

MAKES **2** SERVINGS.

Active Minutes: **30**

Total: **40 minutes**

Per Serving: 276 calories; 10 g fat (1 g sat, 5 g mono); 65 mg cholesterol; 8 g carbohydrate; 27 g protein; 1 g fiber; 232 mg sodium; 500 mg potassium.

Nutrition Bonus: Selenium (40% daily value).

Healthy ╳ Weight

Lower ⬇ Carbs

Tips for Two
CHICKEN BROTH
STORAGE: Leftover canned broth keeps for up to 5 days in the refrigerator or up to 3 months in your freezer. Leftover broths in aseptic packages keep for up to 1 week in the refrigerator. USES: Add to soups, sauces and stews; use for cooking rice and grains; add a little when reheating leftovers to prevent them from drying out.

Marmalade Chicken

Chicken tenders—the strip of rib meat attached to the underside of the chicken breast—are now sold separately, packaged in small amounts. They can help you perform weeknight miracles: they cook in a flash, and unused extras can easily be frozen. Serve this dish with some brown rice (*see page 239*) to soak up the sweet-and-tangy orange sauce.

½ **cup reduced-sodium chicken broth (*see Tips for Two, page 116*)**
1 **tablespoon red-wine vinegar**
1 **tablespoon orange marmalade**
½ **teaspoon Dijon mustard**
½ **teaspoon cornstarch**
8 **ounces chicken tenders**
¼ **teaspoon kosher salt**
⅛ **teaspoon freshly ground pepper**
3 **teaspoons extra-virgin olive oil, divided**
1 **large shallot, minced**
½ **teaspoon freshly grated orange zest**

Active Minutes: **20**

Total: 20 minutes

Per Serving: 213 calories; 8 g fat (1 g sat, 5 g mono); 68 mg cholesterol; 10 g carbohydrate; 27 g protein; 0 g fiber; 246 mg sodium; 55 mg potassium.

Healthy ⋈ Weight

Lower ⬇ Carbs

1. Whisk broth, vinegar, marmalade, mustard and cornstarch in a small bowl.

2. Sprinkle chicken with salt and pepper. Heat 2 teaspoons oil in a medium skillet over medium-high heat. Add the chicken and cook until golden, about 2 minutes per side. Transfer to a plate and cover with foil to keep warm.

3. Add the remaining 1 teaspoon oil and shallot to the pan and cook, stirring often, until the shallot begins to brown, about 30 seconds. Whisk the broth mixture and add it to the pan. Bring to a simmer, scraping up any browned bits with a wooden spoon. Reduce heat to maintain a simmer; cook until the sauce is slightly reduced, 30 seconds to 1 minute. Add the chicken; return to a simmer. Cook, turning once, until the chicken is heated through, about 1 minute. Remove from the heat and stir in orange zest.

MAKES **2** SERVINGS.

Chicken Thighs with Leeks & Shiitakes

Give chicken thighs a quick sauté and finish them with a tarragon-scented sauce. This dish goes well with roasted new potatoes and Lemon Lovers' Asparagus (*page 230*). Look for presliced shiitakes to make preparation of this dish even faster.

- 2 **boneless, skinless chicken thighs, trimmed of fat**
- 1 **tablespoon all-purpose flour**
- 3 **teaspoons extra-virgin olive oil, divided**
- 1 **large leek, white and light green parts only, diced**
- 4 **ounces shiitake mushrooms, stemmed and sliced**
- ½ **cup reduced-sodium chicken broth (*see Tips for Two, page 248*)**
- ¼ **cup dry white wine**
- ⅛ **teaspoon salt**
- 1 **teaspoon minced fresh tarragon *or* ½ teaspoon dried**

1. Place chicken on a plate and sprinkle all over with flour. Reserve the excess flour.

2. Heat 2 teaspoons oil in a large nonstick skillet over medium-high heat. Add the chicken and cook, turning once, until browned on both sides, 4 to 6 minutes total. Transfer to a plate and cover with foil to keep warm.

3. Add the remaining 1 teaspoon oil, leek and mushrooms to the pan. Cook over medium-high heat, stirring often, until the vegetables are tender, 6 to 8 minutes.

4. Sprinkle the reserved flour over the vegetables and stir to coat. Add broth, wine and salt and bring to a simmer. Return the chicken to the pan and simmer, turning the chicken occasionally, until it is cooked through, 4 to 6 minutes. Stir in tarragon.

MAKES **2** SERVINGS.

Active Minutes: **35**

Total: **35 minutes**

Per Serving: 330 calories; 16 g fat (3 g sat, 9 g mono); 77 mg cholesterol; 18 g carbohydrate; 24 g protein; 2 g fiber; 256 mg sodium; 329 mg potassium.

Nutrition Bonus: Selenium (43% daily value), Zinc (20% dv), Vitamin A & Vitamin C (15% dv).

Healthy)(Weight

Lower ⬇ Carbs

CHICKEN, DUCK & TURKEY

Tarragon Chicken

This creamy sauce is a classic with chicken—and while tarragon is the traditional herb, thyme or rosemary would also work beautifully. Serve with sautéed string beans and wild rice.

2   boneless, skinless chicken breasts, trimmed of fat (8 ounces)
¼   teaspoon kosher salt, divided
⅛   teaspoon freshly ground pepper, divided
4   teaspoons extra-virgin olive oil, divided
1   small shallot, finely chopped
¼   cup reduced-sodium chicken broth (*see Tips for Two, page 248*)
¼   cup dry white wine
2   teaspoons Dijon mustard
2   teaspoons reduced-fat sour cream
2   teaspoons chopped fresh tarragon *or* ¾ teaspoon dried

Active Minutes: **30**

Total: 30 minutes

Per Serving: 255 calories; 13 g fat (3 g sat, 8 g mono); 65 mg cholesterol; 4 g carbohydrate; 24 g protein; 0 g fiber; 494 mg sodium; 268 mg potassium.

Nutrition Bonus: Selenium (30% daily value).

Healthy)(**Weight**

Lower ⬇ **Carbs**

1. Season chicken on both sides with ⅛ teaspoon salt and a pinch of pepper. Heat 2 teaspoons oil in a medium nonstick skillet over medium-high heat. Add the chicken and cook until well-browned on both sides, about 3 minutes per side. Transfer to a plate and cover with foil to keep warm.

2. Reduce heat to medium and add the remaining 2 teaspoons oil to the pan. Add shallot and cook, stirring, until softened, about 1 minute. Add broth and wine. Bring to a simmer and cook until reduced by half, 2 to 3 minutes.

3. Return the chicken and any accumulated juices to the pan. Reduce heat and simmer, turning the chicken over halfway through cooking, until the chicken is cooked through, about 4 minutes. Transfer the chicken to 2 plates. Stir mustard, sour cream and tarragon into the sauce. Season with the remaining ⅛ teaspoon salt and the remaining pinch of pepper and spoon over the chicken.

MAKES **2** SERVINGS.

Chicken Tacos with Charred Tomatoes

Charring tomatoes in a hot, dry skillet makes them smoky and flavorful; in combination with fresh herbs and spices, they elevate this dish from "everyday" to "ta-da!" Serve the tacos with reduced-fat sour cream.

Active Minutes: **35**

Total: 35 minutes

Per Serving: 297 calories; 9 g fat (1 g sat, 4 g mono); 63 mg cholesterol; 27 g carbohydrate; 27 g protein; 2 g fiber; 415 mg sodium; 463 mg potassium.

Nutrition Bonus: Selenium & Vitamin C (30% daily value), Vitamin A (20% dv).

Healthy)(Weight

- **2 plum tomatoes, cored**
- **8 ounces boneless, skinless chicken breast, trimmed of fat**
- **¼ teaspoon salt**
- **⅛ teaspoon freshly ground pepper**
- **2 teaspoons canola oil, divided**
- **½ cup finely chopped white onion**
- **1 clove garlic, minced**
- **1 small jalapeño pepper, seeded and minced**
- **2 teaspoons lime juice, plus lime wedges for garnish**
- **2 teaspoons chopped fresh cilantro**
- **2 scallions, chopped**
- **6 small corn tortillas, heated (*see Tip, page 244*)**

1. Heat a medium skillet over high heat until very hot. Add tomatoes and cook, turning occasionally with tongs, until charred on all sides, 8 to 10 minutes. Transfer to a plate to cool slightly. Cut the tomatoes in half crosswise; squeeze to discard seeds and chop the remaining pulp and skin.

2. Cut chicken into 1-inch chunks; sprinkle with salt and pepper. Add 1 teaspoon oil to the pan and heat over high heat until very hot. Add the chicken and cook, stirring occasionally, until it is browned and no longer pink in the middle, 3 to 5 minutes. Transfer to a plate.

3. Reduce the heat to medium and add the remaining 1 teaspoon oil. Add onion and cook, stirring, until softened, about 2 minutes. Add garlic and jalapeño and cook, stirring, until fragrant, about 30 seconds. Add lime juice, the chicken and tomatoes. Cook, stirring, until heated through, 1 to 2 minutes. Stir in cilantro and scallions. Divide the chicken mixture among tortillas. Serve with lime wedges.

MAKES **2** SERVINGS.

Chicken Parmesan Sub

"Sub"? "Hoagie"? "Grinder"? "Hero"? It depends on where you grew up. But we can all agree that the addition of spinach, and the omission of a greasy fried breading, give this old-school favorite a deliciously healthy profile.

- ¼ **cup all-purpose flour**
- ¼ **teaspoon kosher salt**
- ½ **teaspoon freshly ground pepper**
- 2 **boneless, skinless chicken breasts, trimmed of fat (8 ounces)**
- 3 **teaspoons extra-virgin olive oil, divided**
- 1 **6-ounce bag spinach**
- ⅓ **cup prepared marinara sauce (*see Tips for Two*)**
- 2 **tablespoons grated Parmesan cheese**
- ¼ **cup shredded part-skim mozzarella cheese**
- 2 **soft whole-wheat sandwich rolls, toasted**

1. Combine flour, salt and pepper in a shallow dish. Place chicken between two large pieces of plastic wrap. Pound with the smooth side of a meat mallet or a heavy saucepan until the chicken is an even ¼-inch thickness. Dredge the chicken in the flour mixture.

2. Heat 1 teaspoon oil in a large nonstick skillet over medium-high heat. Add spinach, and cook, stirring often, until wilted, 1 to 2 minutes. Transfer to a small bowl.

3. Add the remaining 2 teaspoons oil to the pan. Add the chicken, and cook until golden on first side, 2 to 3 minutes. Turn the chicken, reduce heat to medium, top with the wilted spinach, marinara sauce and Parmesan. Sprinkle with mozzarella, cover and cook until the cheese is melted and the chicken is cooked through, 2 to 3 minutes. Serve on rolls.

MAKES **2** SERVINGS.

Active Minutes: **25**

Total: **25 minutes**

Per Serving: **458 calories; 16 g fat (3 g sat, 8 g mono); 65 mg cholesterol; 45 g carbohydrate; 38 g protein; 4 g fiber; 655 mg sodium; 672 mg potassium.**

Nutrition Bonus: **Vitamin A (160% daily value), Vitamin C (45% dv), Folate (42% dv), Magnesium (23% dv).**

Tips for Two

MARINARA SAUCE

STORAGE: Refrigerate for up to 1 week or freeze for up to 3 months.

USES: Spread on toasted whole-wheat English muffin halves and top with cheese for a quick snack; use for making lasagna; toss with roasted eggplant or other roasted vegetables.

Pollo Cubano

Herb-rolled chicken breasts poached in a flavorful broth make an elegant presentation when sliced and served with lime wedges. Expand on the Caribbean theme by serving this dish with rice and Sautéed Plantains (*page 232*).

Active Minutes: **25**

Total: **40 minutes**

Equipment: Kitchen string

Per Serving: 131 calories; 3 g fat (1 g sat, 1 g mono); 63 mg cholesterol; 2 g carbohydrate; 23 g protein; 0 g fiber; 201 mg sodium; 233 mg potassium.

Nutrition Bonus: Selenium (28% daily value).

Healthy ⋈ Weight

Lower ⬇ Carbs

- **1**   **shallot, minced**
- **3**   **teaspoons chopped fresh cilantro, divided**
- **3**   **teaspoons chopped fresh tarragon, divided**
- **¼**   **teaspoon salt, divided**
- **¼**   **teaspoon freshly ground pepper, divided**
- **2**   **boneless, skinless chicken breasts, trimmed of fat (8 ounces)**
- **2**   **cups water**
- **¼**   **cup lime juice, plus lime wedges for garnish**
- **¼**   **cup dry sherry (*see Note, page 247*)**
- **1½**   **teaspoons crushed red pepper**

1. Combine shallot, 1 teaspoon cilantro, 1 teaspoon tarragon, ⅛ teaspoon salt and ⅛ teaspoon pepper in a small bowl. Divide the mixture evenly and spread along one short end of each breast; roll the chicken up. Secure each roll with kitchen twine by tying one piece horizontally and one piece vertically.

2. Combine the remaining 2 teaspoons cilantro, the remaining 2 teaspoons tarragon, the remaining ⅛ teaspoon salt, the remaining ⅛ teaspoon pepper, water, lime juice, sherry and crushed red pepper in a medium saucepan. Add the chicken rolls and bring to a boil. Cover, reduce heat to low and simmer gently until cooked through and no longer pink in the middle, 10 to 12 minutes.

3. Remove the chicken from the pot and transfer to a cutting board. Let rest 5 minutes. Remove the kitchen string and thinly slice the chicken. Serve with lime wedges.

MAKES **2** SERVINGS.

Miso Chicken Stir-Fry

There's sour, sweet, salty and bitter... and then there's "umami." That's the Japanese term for the "fifth" taste sensation, a delicious meaty or savory taste. This taste comes from glutamates, and can be found in anchovies, soy sauce, fish sauce and tomatoes. This dish, made with miso (fermented soybean paste) is, to use our term, "umami-licious."

- **¼ cup reduced-sodium chicken broth (*see Tips for Two, page 248*)**
- **3 tablespoons miso, preferably white (*see Note, page 246*)**
- **2 tablespoons rice vinegar**
- **1 tablespoon mirin (*see Note*)**
- **2 teaspoons minced fresh ginger**
- **1 teaspoon canola oil**
- **8 ounces boneless, skinless chicken breast, trimmed of fat and thinly sliced**
- **1 cup thinly sliced carrots**
- **¼ cup water**
- **1 medium red bell pepper, thinly sliced**
- **1 cup frozen peas, thawed**

1. Combine broth, miso, vinegar, mirin and ginger in a small bowl.

2. Heat oil in a large nonstick skillet over medium-high heat. Add chicken and cook, stirring occasionally, until browned and cooked through, about 3 minutes. Transfer to a plate.

3. Add carrots and water to the pan; cover and cook, stirring occasionally, until tender-crisp, about 2 minutes. Stir in the miso mixture, bell pepper, peas and the chicken. Cook, stirring occasionally, until the peas are heated through and the sauce is slightly thickened, 1 to 2 minutes.

MAKES 2 SERVINGS, ABOUT 2 CUPS EACH.

Active Minutes: **25**

Total: **25 minutes**

Per Serving: 302 calories; 6 g fat (1 g sat, 2 g mono); 63 mg cholesterol; 29 g carbohydrate; 28 g protein; 7 g fiber; 775 mg sodium; 601 mg potassium.

Nutrition Bonus: Vitamin A (280% daily value), Vitamin C (210% dv), Selenium (30% dv), Potassium (17% dv).

Healthy)(Weight

High ⬆ Fiber

Ingredient Note:

- Mirin is a low-alcohol rice wine essential to Japanese cooking. Look for it in the Asian or gourmet-ingredients section of your supermarket. An equal portion of sherry or white wine with a pinch of sugar may be substituted for mirin.

Stir-Fried Chile-Garlic Duck

Once you turn on the stove, this dish is finished in minutes, so have your ingredients prepped and ready to go. Serve with steamed rice or rice noodles and an iced green tea.

Active Minutes: **30**

Total: 30 minutes

Per Serving: 247 calories; 12 g fat (2 g sat, 6 g mono); 87 mg cholesterol; 10 g carbohydrate; 26 g protein; 3 g fiber; 550 mg sodium; 714 mg potassium.

Nutrition Bonus: Vitamin C (120% daily value), Vitamin A (80% dv), Iron (35% dv), Potassium (20% dv).

Healthy)(Weight

Lower ↓ Carbs

Ingredient Note:

- Chile-garlic sauce, a blend of ground chiles, garlic and vinegar, is commonly used to add heat and flavor to Asian dishes. It can be found in the Asian section of large markets (sometimes labeled as chili-garlic sauce or paste) and keeps up to 1 year in the refrigerator.

1 tablespoon chile-garlic sauce (*see Note*)
1 tablespoon water
1 1/2 teaspoons rice vinegar
1 teaspoon reduced-sodium soy sauce
1/2 teaspoon cornstarch
1 tablespoon canola oil
8 ounces boneless duck breast (*see Note, page 137*) *or* chicken breast, skin removed and cut into 1/4-inch strips
2 cloves garlic, finely chopped
1 tablespoon finely chopped fresh ginger
1 1/2 cups broccoli florets
1 1/2 cups sliced bok choy
1/2 cup sliced shiitake mushrooms (1 ounce)

1. Whisk chile-garlic sauce, water, vinegar, soy sauce and cornstarch in a small bowl.

2. Heat oil in a medium nonstick skillet over medium-high heat until shimmering but not smoking. Cook the duck, in a single layer, stirring once, until beginning to brown, about 3 minutes. Transfer to a plate.

3. Add garlic and ginger to the pan and cook, stirring constantly, until fragrant, about 30 seconds. Add broccoli and bok choy; cook, stirring, until the broccoli is bright green, about 2 minutes. Add mushrooms and cook, stirring, until softened, about 1 minute. Add the chile-garlic sauce mixture; cook, stirring often, until the sauce is slightly thickened, about 1 minute. Return the duck and any accumulated juices to the pan; stir to coat with the sauce. Cook until heated through, about 1 minute.

MAKES **2** SERVINGS, **1** 1/2 CUPS EACH.

Five-Spice Duck Stir-Fry

Why duck? Because it's delicious. This recipe may indeed convince folks who have been tentative about eating duck that they've been missing something fabulous. The five-spice powder, while not overpowering, is strong enough to stand up to the rich taste of duck.

- ¼ cup dry sherry (*see Note, page 247*)
- 2 tablespoons plum sauce
- ¼ teaspoon salt
  Pinch of cayenne pepper
- 1 tablespoon canola oil
- 8 ounces boneless duck breast (*see Note*), skin removed, sliced in half lengthwise, then cut into ¼-inch thick slices
- 2 tablespoons minced garlic
- 2 teaspoons minced fresh ginger
- 1½ cups trimmed, halved green beans
- 2 cups purchased julienne-cut carrots (8 ounces)
- ¼ teaspoon five-spice powder, *or to taste* (*see Note, page 246*)

1. Combine sherry, plum sauce, salt and cayenne in a small bowl.

2. Heat oil in a large nonstick skillet over medium-high heat. Add duck; cook, stirring often, until browned, 1 to 3 minutes. Transfer to a plate with a slotted spatula.

3. Add garlic and ginger to the pan and cook, stirring constantly, until fragrant, about 30 seconds. Add green beans, carrots and five-spice powder, and cook, stirring, until the carrots are slightly softened, about 1 minute. Add the plum sauce mixture; stir to coat, cover, reduce heat to medium and cook until the green beans are tender, 3 to 4 minutes. Add the cooked duck, toss to combine and serve immediately.

MAKES 2 SERVINGS, 1½ CUPS EACH.

Active Minutes: **40**

Total: 40 minutes

Per Serving: 336 calories; 12 g fat (2 g sat, 6 g mono); 87 mg cholesterol; 26 g carbohydrate; 26 g protein; 6 g fiber; 537 mg sodium; 885 mg potassium.

Nutrition Bonus: Vitamin A (390% daily value), Vitamin C (45% dv), Iron (35% dv), Potassium (25% dv), Folate (19% dv).

Healthy ⧓ Weight

Lower ⬇ Carbs

High ⬆ Fiber

CHICKEN, DUCK & TURKEY

Ingredient Note:

- Boneless duck breast halves range widely in weight, from about ½ to 1 pound, depending on the breed. They can be found in most supermarkets in the poultry or specialty-meat sections.

Pomegranate Duck

Duck breasts may seem too fancy for the average weeknight, but they roast up beautifully and quickly. This preparation, with its luscious ruby-colored sauce, is definitely one that will impress. Serve with Herbed Whole-Wheat Couscous (*page 228*).

1	pound boneless duck breast, skin removed (*see Note, page 246*)
½	teaspoon kosher salt
2	teaspoons extra-virgin olive oil
1	small shallot, finely chopped
1	cup pomegranate juice
¼	cup reduced-sodium chicken broth (*see Tips for Two, page 248*)
1	teaspoon cornstarch
2	teaspoons chopped fresh parsley for garnish (optional)

1. Preheat oven to 450°F.

2. Sprinkle duck with salt. Heat oil in a medium skillet over medium-high heat. Add the duck and cook until browned on both sides, 3 to 4 minutes per side. Transfer the duck to a small baking dish and roast until a thermometer inserted into the thickest part registers 150°F, 8 to 12 minutes for medium, depending on the size of the breast. Transfer to a cutting board; let rest 5 minutes.

3. While the duck is roasting, return the pan to medium-high heat. Add shallot and cook, stirring constantly, until fragrant, 30 seconds to 1 minute. Add pomegranate juice and bring to a boil. Reduce heat to a simmer; cook until reduced by half, 1 to 2 minutes. Stir broth and cornstarch in a small bowl until the cornstarch dissolves. Add to the pan. Bring to a boil, stirring constantly. Reduce heat to a simmer and cook, stirring, until the sauce is thickened, 1 to 2 minutes. When the duck has finished resting, pour any accumulated juices into the sauce and stir to combine.

4. Thinly slice the duck; serve topped with the pomegranate sauce. Garnish with parsley, if desired.

MAKES **2** SERVINGS.

Active Minutes: **45**

Total: **45 minutes**

Per Serving: 272 calories; 10 g fat (2 g sat, 5 g mono); 88 mg cholesterol; 22 g carbohydrate; 23 g protein; 0 g fiber; 368 mg sodium; 552 mg potassium.

Nutrition Bonus: Iron (30% daily value), Potassium (16% dv), Vitamin C (15% dv).

Healthy ✗ Weight

Lower ⬇ Carbs

CHICKEN, DUCK & TURKEY

Turkey & Stuffing

Thanksgiving in a skillet. Leftover homemade corn muffins are perfect for the stuffing, but if you don't have any, pick one up at the supermarket bakery or your local coffee shop.

Active Minutes: **35**

Total: **35 minutes**

Per Serving: **496 calories; 15 g fat (4 g sat, 9 g mono); 63 mg cholesterol; 48 g carbohydrate; 33 g protein; 3 g fiber; 593 mg sodium; 187 mg potassium.**

Nutrition Bonus: Iron (15% daily value).

4 teaspoons extra-virgin olive oil, divided
1 small onion, chopped
1 stalk celery, sliced
2 small, homemade corn muffins *or* 1 large store-bought corn muffin, crumbled
1 tablespoon minced fresh sage *or* 1 teaspoon dried rubbed sage
¼ cup dried cranberries
1 cup reduced-sodium chicken broth (*see Tips for Two, page 248*), divided
8 ounces turkey cutlets
⅛ teaspoon salt
¼ teaspoon freshly ground pepper
¼ cup all-purpose flour
½ cup dry white wine
1 teaspoon Dijon mustard

1. ◆ Heat 2 teaspoons oil in a large nonstick skillet over medium heat. Add onion and celery. Cover and cook, stirring occasionally, until softened, about 4 minutes. Add corn muffin and cook, stirring often, until lightly toasted, about 3 minutes. Add sage, cranberries and ½ cup broth and cook, stirring, until heated through, about 2 minutes. Transfer the mixture to a medium bowl and cover with foil to keep warm. Wash and dry the pan.

2. ◆ Season turkey with salt and pepper. Place flour in a shallow dish and dredge the turkey in it. Heat the remaining 2 teaspoons oil in the pan over medium-high heat. Add the turkey and cook until golden and cooked through, 2 to 3 minutes per side. Transfer to a plate and cover with foil to keep warm.

3. ◆ Return the pan to medium-high heat. Add the remaining ½ cup broth, wine and mustard. Cook, scraping up any browned bits, until slightly reduced, 2 to 4 minutes. Serve the sauce over the stuffing and turkey.

MAKES **2** SERVINGS.

Turkey Scallopini with Apricot Sauce

Nectar (juice by any other name) makes a sweet-and-sour sauce that also pairs well with pork chops or chicken. The orange elements in this dish beg for another vibrant color—perhaps steamed broccoli and red bell pepper—on the side.

2	tablespoons all-purpose flour
1/4	teaspoon salt
1/4	teaspoon freshly ground pepper
8	ounces turkey cutlets
2	teaspoons canola oil
1 1/2	tablespoons minced shallot *or* onion
1 1/2	teaspoons minced fresh ginger
1/3	cup apricot *or* peach nectar (*see Tips for Two*)
1/3	cup reduced-sodium chicken broth (*see Tips for Two, page 248*)
1	tablespoon cider vinegar *or* white-wine vinegar
1/2	teaspoon brown sugar
2	tablespoons chopped dried apricots
1	teaspoon chopped fresh mint *or* 1/4 teaspoon dried

1. Combine flour, salt and pepper in a shallow dish. Dredge turkey in the flour mixture.

2. Heat oil in a medium nonstick skillet over medium-high heat. Add the turkey and cook until golden and cooked through, 2 to 3 minutes per side. Transfer to a plate and cover with foil to keep warm.

3. Add shallot (or onion) and ginger to the pan. Cook, stirring, until fragrant, about 30 seconds. Add nectar, broth, vinegar and sugar; bring to a boil, stirring. Add apricots and cook until the apricots are tender and the sauce has reduced slightly, 2 to 3 minutes. Remove from the heat and stir in mint. Spoon the sauce over the turkey.

MAKES **2** SERVINGS.

Active Minutes: **30**

Total: 30 minutes

Per Serving: 239 calories; 5 g fat (0 g sat, 3 g mono); 46 mg cholesterol; 18 g carbohydrate; 30 g protein; 1 g fiber; 329 mg sodium; 189 mg potassium.

Nutrition Bonus: Vitamin A (20% daily value), Vitamin C (15% dv).

Healthy ⟩⟨ Weight

Lower ⬇ Carbs

Tips for Two

APRICOT NECTAR

STORAGE: Refrigerate for up to 1 week .

USES: Add to smoothies; whisk into salad dressing; combine with sparkling water for a refreshing non-alcoholic beverage.

Turkey Fingers with Maple-Mustard Sauce

Feel like a kid again—okay, a health-conscious kid—with crispy, crunchy oven "fried" turkey fingers and a sweet and savory dipping sauce. To save time, make the sauce ahead or while the tenders are baking. Serve with Oven Sweet Potato Fries (*page 230*).

Active Minutes: **25**

Total: **40 minutes**

Per Serving: 340 calories; 5 g fat (0 g sat, 0 g mono); 46 mg cholesterol; 44 g carbohydrate; 34 g protein; 4 g fiber; 742 mg sodium; 164 mg potassium.

Nutrition Bonus: Iron (20% daily value).

Cooking spray
½ **cup buttermilk**
1 **teaspoon whole-grain mustard**
⅓ **cup yellow cornmeal**
¼ **cup all-purpose flour**
½ **teaspoon ground cumin**
½ **teaspoon dried thyme**
¼ **teaspoon salt**
8 **ounces turkey breast, such as tenderloin, cutlets *or* boneless breast chops, cut into finger-size strips**
Maple-Mustard Sauce (*page 226*)

1. Set oven rack at lowest position and preheat to 450°F. Coat a rimmed baking sheet with cooking spray.

2. Whisk buttermilk and mustard in a medium bowl. Combine cornmeal, flour, cumin, thyme and salt in a shallow dish. Dip turkey into the buttermilk mixture then dredge in the cornmeal mixture.

3. Place the prepared baking sheet in the oven for 5 minutes. Place the turkey fingers on the hot baking sheet and coat on all sides with cooking spray. Bake until the bottoms of the fingers are golden, about 10 minutes. Turn the fingers over and bake until golden brown on the outside and no longer pink in the middle, 8 to 10 minutes more.

4. While the turkey fingers are baking, prepare Maple-Mustard Sauce. Serve the turkey fingers with the sauce for dipping.

MAKES **2** SERVINGS.

Turkey Marsala

Mushrooms of any type may be used in this elegant dish. Nutty-tasting, oven-roasted Brussels sprouts (*page 234*) make a great side, as does quick-cooking barley or some brown rice (*see page 239*).

Active Minutes: 25

Total: 25 minutes

Per Serving: 214 calories; 8 g fat (1 g sat, 4 g mono); 46 mg cholesterol; 7 g carbohydrate; 31 g protein; 1 g fiber; 206 mg sodium; 368 mg potassium.

Nutrition Bonus: Selenium (16% daily value).

Healthy)(Weight

Lower ⬇ Carbs

- **2** **tablespoons all-purpose flour**
- **1/4** **teaspoon salt**
- **1/8** **teaspoon freshly ground pepper**
- **8** **ounces turkey cutlets**
- **3** **teaspoons canola oil, divided**
- **3** **cups thinly sliced, mixed mushrooms, such as shiitake, oyster, chanterelle, white *or* cremini (6 ounces)**
- **1/4** **cup Marsala (*see Note, page 246*)**
- **1/4** **cup reduced-sodium chicken broth (*see Tips for Two, page 248*)**
- **1** **teaspoon chopped fresh parsley**

1. Whisk flour, salt and pepper in a shallow dish. Dredge turkey in the flour mixture.

2. Heat 2 teaspoons oil in a medium nonstick skillet over medium heat. Add the turkey and cook until just beginning to color, about 2 minutes per side. Transfer to a plate and cover with foil to keep warm.

3. Increase heat to medium-high. Add the remaining 1 teaspoon oil and mushrooms; cook, stirring often, until softened, 2 to 4 minutes. Cover, reduce heat to low and cook, stirring occasionally, until the mushrooms are tender, 2 to 4 minutes.

4. Increase heat to medium-high, add Marsala and broth; bring to a boil. Cook, stirring with a wooden spoon to scrape up any browned bits, until the sauce thickens slightly, 1 to 2 minutes. Reduce heat to medium-low, return the turkey to the pan. Cook, turning once, until the turkey is heated through, 1 to 2 minutes. Serve garnished with parsley.

MAKES **2** SERVINGS.

Turkey Cutlets with Lemon-Caper Sauce

L emon, capers and parsley are a commonly grouped trio. The sauce is also good with chicken breasts, fish fillets or veal cutlets. This recipe really keeps the fat in check by using water in the skillet to keep the onions moist while sautéing.

- **2 tablespoons all-purpose flour**
- **¼ teaspoon freshly ground pepper**
- **8 ounces turkey cutlets**
- **2 teaspoons extra-virgin olive oil**
- **1 small onion, finely chopped**
- **½ teaspoon minced fresh thyme**
- **1 tablespoon water**
- **1 cup reduced-sodium chicken broth (*see Tips for Two, page 248*)**
- **1 tablespoon capers, rinsed and roughly chopped**
- **1 tablespoon lemon juice**
- **1 tablespoon finely chopped fresh parsley**

1. ❖ Combine flour and pepper in a shallow dish. Dredge turkey in the flour mixture. Reserve 2 teaspoons of the flour mixture.

2. ❖ Heat oil in a medium nonstick skillet over medium-high heat. Add the turkey and cook until browned on both sides, 2 to 3 minutes per side. Transfer to a plate and cover with foil to keep warm.

3. ❖ Add onion, thyme and water to the pan. Cook, stirring often, until the onions are slightly softened, about 3 minutes. Sprinkle with the reserved flour mixture; stir to coat. Add broth and bring to a simmer, stirring constantly. Cook until the onion is softened, about 3 minutes. Add capers, lemon juice and parsley to the sauce. Return the turkey to the pan. Cook, turning once, until heated through, about 1 minute.

MAKES **2** SERVINGS.

Active Minutes: **25**

Total: 25 minutes

Per Serving: 220 calories; 6 g fat (1 g sat, 4 g mono); 48 mg cholesterol; 11 g carbohydrate; 31 g protein; 1 g fiber; 300 mg sodium; 81 mg potassium.

Nutrition Bonus: Vitamin C (15% daily value).

Healthy)(Weight

Lower ⬇ Carbs

CHICKEN, DUCK & TURKEY

Sweet & Savory Cutlets

Miso is usually associated with Japanese cuisine, but here we've appropriated it to lend a decidedly un-Japanese sauce a rich taste. Garnish with fresh parsley and serve with brown basmati rice.

Active Minutes: **30**

Total: 30 minutes

Per Serving: 334 calories; 11 g fat (1 g sat, 7 g mono); 45 mg cholesterol; 25 g carbohydrate; 32 g protein; 2 g fiber; 430 mg sodium; 479 mg potassium.

Nutrition Bonus: Vitamin C (30% daily value), Iron (15% dv).

Healthy)(Weight

½	cup water
¼	cup orange juice
2	tablespoons dry sherry *or* Madeira (*see Note, page 247*)
1	tablespoon miso, preferably dark (*see Note, page 246*)
4	pitted prunes, diced
½	teaspoon dried rosemary
2	tablespoons all-purpose flour
8	ounces turkey cutlets
⅛	teaspoon salt
⅛	teaspoon freshly ground pepper
4	teaspoons extra-virgin olive oil, divided
1	small shallot, chopped
4	ounces white *or* cremini mushrooms, thickly sliced (2 cups)

1. Combine water, orange juice, sherry (or Madeira) and miso in a medium bowl; whisk until smooth. Add prunes and rosemary; set aside.

2. Place flour in a shallow dish. Season turkey with salt and pepper and lightly dredge in the flour, shaking off excess.

3. Heat 2 teaspoons oil in a medium skillet over medium-high heat. Add the turkey and cook until golden, about 2 minutes per side. Transfer to a plate and cover with foil to keep warm.

4. Heat the remaining 2 teaspoons oil in the pan over medium heat. Add shallot and mushrooms; cook, stirring, until browned, 3 to 5 minutes. Add the miso mixture; cook, stirring, until slightly thickened, 2 to 3 minutes.

5. Reduce heat to low and return the turkey and any accumulated juices to the pan. Simmer gently, spooning sauce over turkey, until heated through, about 1 minute.

MAKES **2** SERVINGS.

Turkey & Fontina Melts

An elegant presentation of turkey layered with spinach and cheese, yet surprisingly quick to make. Round out the meal with a side of whole-wheat pasta, a salad and a glass of Pinot Noir.

- **2 turkey cutlets (8 ounces)**
- **1 tablespoon all-purpose flour**
- **3 teaspoons extra-virgin olive oil, divided**
- **1 large shallot, minced**
- **¼ cup dry sherry (*see Note, page 247*)**
- **1 6-ounce bag baby spinach**
- **¼ cup finely shredded Fontina cheese**
- **1 teaspoon butter**

1. Position rack in the upper third of the oven; preheat broiler.

2. Sprinkle both sides of turkey with flour. Heat 2 teaspoons oil in a medium ovenproof skillet over medium-high heat. Add the turkey and cook until golden, about 2 minutes per side. Transfer the turkey to a plate.

3. Add the remaining 1 teaspoon oil and shallot to the pan; cook, stirring constantly, until lightly browned, 1 to 2 minutes. Add sherry and spinach; cook, stirring constantly, until the spinach is wilted, 1 to 2 minutes. Remove from the heat.

4. Carefully mound equal portions of the spinach on top of the turkey. Transfer the spinach-topped turkey and any accumulated juices to the pan. Top the spinach with cheese and transfer to the oven. Broil until the cheese is melted, 1 to 2 minutes.

5. Transfer the melts to 2 plates. Add the butter to the pan and whisk into the juices over medium-high heat until melted, about 30 seconds. Drizzle over the melts.

MAKES **2** SERVINGS.

Active Minutes: **15**

Total: **20 minutes**

Per Serving: 332 calories; 14 g fat (5 g sat, 7 g mono); 66 mg cholesterol; 15 g carbohydrate; 34 g protein; 4 g fiber; 347 mg sodium; 89 mg potassium.

Nutrition Bonus: **Vitamin A (70% daily value), Iron (25% dv), Vitamin C (20% dv), Calcium (15% dv).**

Healthy ✕ Weight

Lower ⬇ Carbs

CHICKEN, DUCK & TURKEY

Fennel Sauerkraut with Sausage & Potatoes

Inspired by the Alsatian classic *choucroute garni*, this comforting, one-pot meal takes a shortcut with bagged shredded cabbage. Serve topped with additional brown mustard, if you like.

Active Minutes: **30**

Total: **35 minutes**

Per Serving: 311 calories; 14 g fat (4 g sat, 4 g mono); 52 mg cholesterol; 28 g carbohydrate; 19 g protein; 7 g fiber; 825 mg sodium; 731 mg potassium.

Nutrition Bonus: Vitamin C (90% daily value), Potassium (21% dv), Iron (20% dv).

Healthy){ Weight

High ⬆ Fiber

Tips for Two

CABBAGE

STORAGE: Refrigerate for up to 1 week.
USES: Add to salads or soup; Vinegary Coleslaw (*page 227*) or Warm Apple-Cabbage Slaw (*page 228*).

2	teaspoons extra-virgin olive oil, divided
6	ounces sweet Italian turkey sausage links
¾	cup ½-inch diced red potatoes
2	cups packaged shredded cabbage, preferably "angel hair" style (*see Tips for Two*)
1	small bulb fennel, quartered, cored and thinly sliced, plus 1 tablespoon chopped feathery tops
1	small onion, sliced
½	teaspoon garlic powder
½	teaspoon fennel seed
½	teaspoon freshly ground pepper
½	cup reduced-sodium chicken broth (*see Tips for Two, page 248*)
2	tablespoons white-wine vinegar
1½	teaspoons brown *or* whole-grain mustard

1. Heat 1 teaspoon oil in a large skillet over medium-high heat. Add sausage and cook, turning often, until lightly browned, about 3 minutes. Transfer the sausage to a cutting board and slice into ½-inch pieces. (The sausage will not be thoroughly cooked, but it will continue cooking later.)

2. Add the remaining 1 teaspoon oil to the pan and heat over medium heat. Add potatoes and cook, stirring occasionally, for 3 minutes. Add cabbage, sliced fennel, onion, garlic powder, fennel seed and pepper. Cook, stirring often, until the cabbage has wilted slightly, about 3 minutes more.

3. Add broth, vinegar and mustard. Stir to incorporate the mustard; bring to a simmer. Place the sausage on top of the cabbage mixture; cover, reduce heat to medium-low and cook until the sausage is cooked through and the vegetables are tender, 7 to 10 minutes. Stir in chopped fennel fronds and serve.

MAKES **2** SERVINGS.

CHAPTER 5

Fish & Seafood

Broiled Salmon with Miso Glaze

Combine miso (fermented soybean paste), mirin (Japanese rice wine), soy sauce and ginger, and you get a rich and delectable Japanese-style glaze for salmon (or chicken, tofu, pork chops, etc.). These versatile ingredients last for months in the refrigerator and add incomparable flavor.

Active Minutes: **15**

Total: **25 minutes**

Per Serving: 214 calories; 9 g fat (1 g sat, 3 g mono); 62 mg cholesterol; 7 g carbohydrate; 24 g protein; 1 g fiber; 421 mg sodium; 603 mg potassium.

Nutrition Bonus: Selenium (60% daily value), high omega-3s.

Healthy ✕ Weight

Lower ⬇ Carbs

Tip:

- To toast sesame seeds, heat a small dry skillet over low heat. Add sesame seeds and stir constantly until golden and fragrant, about 2 minutes. Transfer to a small bowl and let cool.

1	tablespoon miso, preferably white (*see Note, page 246*)
1	tablespoon mirin (*see Note, page 246*)
1 ½	teaspoons reduced-sodium soy sauce
1 ½	teaspoons minced fresh ginger
	Hot pepper sauce to taste
8	ounces center-cut salmon fillet, skinned (*see Tip, page 245*) and cut into 2 portions
1	tablespoon thinly sliced scallions
1	tablespoon chopped fresh cilantro
1 ½	teaspoons toasted sesame seeds (*see Tip*)

1. Position rack in upper third of oven; preheat broiler. Line a small baking pan with foil. Coat the foil with cooking spray.

2. Whisk miso, mirin, soy sauce, ginger and hot sauce in a small bowl until smooth.

3. Place salmon fillets, skinned-side down, in the prepared pan. Brush generously with the miso mixture. Broil the salmon until just cooked through in the center, 6 to 8 minutes. Garnish the salmon with scallions, cilantro and sesame seeds.

MAKES **2** SERVINGS.

Poached Salmon with Creamy Piccata Sauce

Simple poached salmon is anything but bland when topped with this piquant sauce. Serve with roasted asparagus, sliced fresh tomatoes and some crusty, garlic-rubbed, toasted farm bread.

8   ounces center-cut salmon fillet, skinned (*see Tip, page 245*) and cut into 2 portions
½   cup dry white wine, divided
1   teaspoon extra-virgin olive oil
1   small shallot, minced
1   tablespoon lemon juice
2   teaspoons capers, rinsed
2   tablespoons reduced-fat sour cream
⅛   teaspoon salt
2   teaspoons chopped fresh dill

1. Place salmon in a medium skillet. Add ¼ cup wine and enough water to just cover the salmon. Bring to a boil over high heat. Reduce to a simmer, turn the salmon over, cover and cook for 5 minutes. Remove from the heat.

2. Meanwhile, heat oil in a small skillet over medium-high heat. Add shallot and cook, stirring, until fragrant, about 30 seconds. Add the remaining ¼ cup wine; boil until slightly reduced, about 1 minute. Stir in lemon juice and capers and cook 1 minute more. Remove from the heat, stir in sour cream and salt. Serve the salmon topped with the sauce and garnished with dill.

MAKES **2** SERVINGS.

Active Minutes: **20**

Total: 20 minutes

Per Serving: 281 calories; 16 g fat (4 g sat, 7 g mono); 73 mg cholesterol; 3 g carbohydrate; 23 g protein; 0 g fiber; 306 mg sodium; 486 mg potassium.

Nutrition Bonus: Selenium (60% daily value), Vitamin C (15% dv), high omega-3s.

Healthy)(Weight

Lower ⬇ Carbs

Salsa-Roasted Salmon

Fire up the food processor, add a few simple ingredients, and you've got a vibrant-tasting salsa in minutes. Other fish and even chicken or turkey could stand in for the salmon—adjust the roasting time accordingly.

1	medium plum tomato, roughly chopped
1/2	small onion, roughly chopped
1	clove garlic, peeled and quartered
1	small jalapeño pepper, seeded and roughly chopped
1	teaspoon cider vinegar
1/2	teaspoon chili powder
1/4	teaspoon ground cumin
1/4	teaspoon salt
2-3	dashes hot sauce
8	ounces center-cut salmon fillet, skinned (*see Tip, page 245*) and cut into 2 portions

1. Preheat oven to 400°F.

2. Place tomato, onion, garlic, jalapeño, vinegar, chili powder, cumin, salt and hot sauce to taste in a food processor; process until finely chopped and uniform.

3. Place salmon in a medium roasting pan; spoon the salsa on top. Roast until the salmon is just cooked through, 12 to 15 minutes.

MAKES **2** SERVINGS.

Active Minutes: **10**

Total: **25 minutes**

To Make Ahead: The salsa (Step 2) will keep, covered, in the refrigerator for up to 1 day.

Per Serving: 229 calories; 13 g fat (3 g sat, 4 g mono); 67 mg cholesterol; 4 g carbohydrate; 23 g protein; 1 g fiber; 376 mg sodium; 548 mg potassium.

Nutrition Bonus: Selenium (60% daily value), Vitamin C (20% dv), Potassium (16% dv), Vitamin A (15% dv).

Healthy ⚓ Weight

Lower ⬇ Carbs

Moroccan Grilled Salmon

Tangy plain yogurt mixed with the classic ingredients for *chermoula*—a Moroccan spice mix—serves as both the marinade and the sauce in this recipe. If you like your food on the spicy side, add a pinch of cayenne to the mixture.

Active Minutes: **20**

Total: 40 minutes

Per Serving: 290 calories; 20 g fat (4 g sat, 10 g mono); 68 mg cholesterol; 2 g carbohydrate; 23 g protein; 0 g fiber; 184 mg sodium; 481 mg potassium.

Nutrition Bonus: Selenium (60% daily value), Vitamin C (20% dv), high omega-3s.

Healthy ⅜ Weight

Lower ⬇ Carbs

2	tablespoons low-fat *or* nonfat plain yogurt
2	tablespoons chopped fresh parsley
2	tablespoons chopped fresh cilantro
1	tablespoon lemon juice
1½	teaspoons extra-virgin olive oil
1	clove garlic, minced
¾	teaspoon paprika
½	teaspoon ground cumin
⅛	teaspoon salt
	Freshly ground pepper to taste
8	ounces center-cut salmon fillet, skinned (*see Tip, page 245*) and cut into 2 portions
2	lemon wedges

1. Combine yogurt, parsley, cilantro, lemon juice, oil, garlic, paprika, cumin, salt and pepper in a small bowl. Reserve 2 tablespoons of the sauce; cover and refrigerate. Place salmon in a medium sealable plastic bag. Pour in the remaining yogurt mixture, seal the bag and turn to coat. Refrigerate for 10 (or up to 30) minutes.

2. Meanwhile, preheat grill to medium-high.

3. Oil the grill rack (*see Tip, page 244*). Remove the salmon from the marinade, blotting any excess. Grill the salmon until it is browned and just cooked through, 4 to 5 minutes per side. Top the salmon with the reserved sauce and garnish with lemon wedges.

MAKES **2** SERVINGS.

Blackened Salmon Po' Boy

Mashed avocado mixed with reduced-fat mayo creates a cool, creamy spread—the perfect counterpoint to the spicy salmon and peppery arugula in this recipe. Catfish is another tasty choice for this sandwich. Serve with Oven Sweet Potato Fries *(page 230)*.

½	**small avocado, pitted (*see Tips for Two*)**
1	**tablespoon reduced-fat mayonnaise**
1	**teaspoon blackening *or* Cajun seasoning**
8	**ounces salmon fillet, skinned (*see Tip, page 245*) and cut into 2 portions**
2	**crusty whole-wheat rolls, split and toasted**
1	**cup arugula**
1	**plum tomato, thinly sliced**
¼	**cup thinly sliced red onion**

1. ◆ Preheat grill to high. Oil grill rack *(see Tip, page 244)*.

2. ◆ Mash together avocado and mayonnaise in a small bowl with a fork.

3. ◆ Rub blackening (or Cajun) seasoning on both sides of salmon. Grill until just cooked through, about 3 to 4 minutes per side.

4. ◆ To assemble the sandwiches, spread the avocado mixture on the bottom half of each roll. Top with the salmon, arugula, tomato and onion.

MAKES **2** SERVINGS.

Active Minutes: **25**

Total: 25 minutes

Per Serving: 431 calories; 16 g fat (3 g sat, 7 g mono); 67 mg cholesterol; 43 g carbohydrate; 33 g protein; 6 g fiber; 756 mg sodium; 774 mg potassium.

Nutrition Bonus: Selenium (78% daily value), Potassium (22% dv), Vitamin C (20% dv), Folate (16% dv).

High ⬆ Fiber

Tips for Two
AVOCADO
STORAGE: Although browning is inevitable, less browning is possible if you keep the pit in the half you're storing and wrap it tightly in plastic wrap.
USES: Mash with reduced-fat mayonnaise and use as a sandwich spread; dice and sprinkle on top of scrambled eggs; toss in salad.

Fennel-Crusted Salmon with White Beans

You could call this recipe triple-fennel salmon because it uses the fresh fennel bulb, the fronds *and* fennel seeds. The end result is melt-in-your-mouth, seared salmon fillets with an earthy bean topping. Add a mesclun salad to complete the meal.

Active Minutes: **30**

Total: 35 minutes

Per Serving: 460 calories; 21 g fat (4 g sat, 10 g mono); 67 mg cholesterol; 39 g carbohydrate; 34 g protein; 13 g fiber; 610 mg sodium; 1,589 mg potassium.

Nutrition Bonus: Vitamin C (50% daily value), Potassium (45% dv), Calcium, Iron & Vitamin A (20% dv), Folate (18% dv).

High ⬆ Fiber

Tip:

- To skin a salmon fillet, place it skin-side down on a cutting board. Starting at one corner, slip the blade of a long, knife between the fish flesh and the skin, holding the skin down firmly with your other hand. Gently push the blade along at a 30° angle, separating the fillet from the skin without cutting through either.

3　teaspoons extra-virgin olive oil, divided
1　small bulb fennel, halved, cored and thinly sliced, plus 1 tablespoon chopped fennel fronds
1　15-ounce can white beans, rinsed
1　medium tomato, diced
1/4　cup dry white wine
1 1/2　teaspoons Dijon mustard
1/4　teaspoon freshly ground pepper, divided
1　teaspoon fennel seed
8　ounces center-cut salmon fillet, skinned (*see Tip*) and cut into 2 portions

1. Heat 1 teaspoon oil in a large nonstick skillet over medium heat. Add sliced fennel; cook, stirring occasionally, until lightly browned, about 6 minutes. Stir in beans, tomato and wine. Cook, stirring occasionally, until the tomato begins to break down, about 3 minutes. Transfer to a bowl; stir in chopped fennel fronds, mustard and 1/8 teaspoon pepper. Cover to keep warm.

2. Rinse and dry the pan. Combine fennel seed and the remaining 1/8 teaspoon pepper in a small bowl; sprinkle evenly on both sides of salmon. Heat the remaining 2 teaspoons oil in the pan over medium-high heat until shimmering but not smoking. Add the salmon, skinned side up; cook until golden brown, 3 to 6 minutes. Turn the salmon over, cover and remove from heat. Allow the salmon to finish cooking off the heat until just cooked through, 3 to 6 minutes more. Serve the salmon with the bean mixture.

MAKES **2** SERVINGS.

Easy Salmon Cakes

Keep canned salmon in the pantry, if only for this delectable recipe. Canned salmon is not only convenient but delicious and heart-healthy. When shopping, look for salmon labeled "boneless," or be prepared to pick out or eat the small bones. Of course, leftover cooked salmon works as well.

- **3 teaspoons extra-virgin olive oil, divided**
- **¼ cup finely chopped onion**
- **⅓ cup finely diced celery**
- **1 tablespoon chopped fresh parsley**
- **7 ounces canned salmon, drained, *or* ¾ cup cooked flaked salmon**
- **1 egg white *or* 2 tablespoons Egg Beaters**
- **¾ teaspoon Dijon mustard**
- **1 cup fresh whole-wheat breadcrumbs (*see Tip, page 244*)**
- **¼ teaspoon freshly ground pepper**
  Creamy Dill Sauce (*page 226*)
- **1 lemon, cut into wedges**

1. Preheat oven to 450°F. Coat a baking sheet with cooking spray.

2. Heat 1 teaspoon oil in a medium nonstick skillet over medium-high heat. Add onion and celery; cook, stirring, until softened, about 3 minutes. Stir in parsley; remove from the heat.

3. Place salmon in a medium bowl. Flake with a fork; remove any bones and skin. Add egg white (or Egg Beaters), mustard and 1 teaspoon oil; mix well. Add the onion mixture, breadcrumbs and pepper; mix well. Shape the mixture into four 2½-inch-wide patties.

4. Heat the remaining 1 teaspoon oil in the pan over medium heat. Add the salmon cakes and cook until the undersides are golden, 2 to 3 minutes. Using a wide spatula, turn them over onto the prepared baking sheet.

5. Bake the salmon cakes until firm and heated through, 10 to 15 minutes. Prepare Creamy Dill Sauce. Serve the cakes with the sauce and lemon wedges.

MAKES **2** SERVINGS.

Active Minutes: **35**

Total: 40 minutes

To Make Ahead: Prepare the cakes (Steps 2 & 3). Cover and refrigerate for up to 8 hours.

Per Serving: 340 calories; 14 g fat (1 g sat, 6 g mono); 78 mg cholesterol; 28 g carbohydrate; 32 g protein; 8 g fiber; 657 mg sodium; 161 mg potassium.

Nutrition Bonus: Vitamin C (30% daily value), Calcium (20% dv), Magnesium (17% dv), Iron (15% dv).

Healthy)(Weight

High ↑ Fiber

Smoked Trout Hash with Mustard Greens

Mustard greens and smoked trout give a flavorful twist to the idea of hash. To make it a satisfying supper, top with a poached egg or serve with sliced ripe tomatoes with cracked black pepper. If you prefer a milder green, use spinach or Swiss chard instead.

Active Minutes: **20**

Total: 20 minutes

Per Serving: 221 calories; 10 g fat (2 g sat, 6 g mono); 22 mg cholesterol; 22 g carbohydrate; 11 g protein; 2 g fiber; 525 mg sodium; 633 mg potassium.

Nutrition Bonus: Vitamin A (120% daily value), Vitamin C (70% dv), Folate (26% dv), Potassium (18% dv).

Healthy)(Weight

Lower ⬇ Carbs

Ingredient Note:

● Look for precooked diced potatoes in the refrigerated section of most supermarket produce departments, near other fresh, prepared vegetables.

1 ½ **tablespoons extra-virgin olive oil**
8 **ounces precooked diced red-skinned potatoes (about 1 ¼ cups; see Note)**
1 **tablespoon whole-grain mustard**
1 **tablespoon cider vinegar**
Pinch of salt, or to taste
Freshly ground pepper to taste
2 **ounces smoked trout, skin removed and flaked (½ cup)**
2 **cups thinly sliced mustard greens**

1. Heat oil in a large nonstick skillet over medium-high heat. Add potatoes; cook, stirring occasionally, until golden and crispy, adjusting heat if necessary, 8 to 12 minutes.

2. Whisk mustard, vinegar, salt and pepper in a small bowl. Add to the potatoes along with trout and greens. Cook, stirring, until the greens are just wilted, 30 seconds to 1 minute. Remove from the heat; stir 1 to 2 tablespoons water into the hash if it seems dry. Serve hot.

MAKES **2** SERVINGS, ABOUT **1** CUP EACH.

Grandma Ginger's Fish Casserole

Recipe developer Katie Webster's grandmother used to make a version of this dish with fresh-caught smallmouth bass from Vermont's Lake Champlain. Our updated version requires no fishing; just a trip to the supermarket for Pacific cod or tilapia.

4	teaspoons extra-virgin olive oil, divided
1	medium onion, very thinly sliced
½	cup dry white wine
8	ounces Pacific cod (*see Note*) *or* tilapia, cut into 2 pieces
1	teaspoon chopped fresh thyme *or* ¼ teaspoon dried
¼	teaspoon kosher salt
¼	teaspoon freshly ground pepper
¾	cup finely chopped whole-wheat country bread (about 1 slice)
¼	teaspoon paprika
¼	teaspoon garlic powder
½	cup finely shredded Gruyère *or* Swiss cheese

1. Preheat oven to 400°F.

2. Heat 2 teaspoons oil in a medium ovenproof skillet over medium-high heat. Add onion and cook, stirring often, until just starting to soften, 4 to 6 minutes. Add wine, increase heat to high and cook, stirring often, until the wine is slightly reduced, 2 to 4 minutes.

3. Place fish on top of the onion and sprinkle with thyme, salt and pepper. Cover the pan tightly with foil; transfer to the oven and bake for 12 minutes.

4. Toss the bread with the remaining 2 teaspoons oil, paprika and garlic powder in a small bowl. Uncover the fish; top with the bread mixture and cheese. Bake, uncovered, until the fish is just cooked through, 8 to 10 minutes.

MAKES **2** SERVINGS.

Active Minutes: **20**

Total: 35 minutes

Per Serving: 383 calories; 19 g fat (7 g sat, 10 g mono); 73 mg cholesterol; 15 g carbohydrate; 28 g protein; 4 g fiber; 337 mg sodium; 346 mg potassium.

Nutrition Bonus: Selenium (48% daily value), Calcium (35% dv), Zinc (20% dv), Magnesium (19% dv).

Lower ⬇ **Carbs**

Ingredient Note:

● Overfishing and trawling have drastically reduced the number of cod in the Atlantic Ocean and destroyed its sea floor. A better choice is Pacific cod (aka Alaska cod); it is more sustainably fished and has a larger, more stable population (mbayaq.org/cr/seafoodwatch.asp).

Thyme- & Sesame-Crusted Pacific Halibut

A speedy roast at high heat keeps the fish moist and succulent. The savory crust adds a distinctive finish. Serve with Buttermilk-Herb Mashed Potatoes (*page 229*) and a steamed fresh vegetable of your choice.

Active Minutes: **10**

Total: **35 minutes**

Per Serving: 225 calories; 12 g fat (2 g sat, 6 g mono); 36 mg cholesterol; 4 g carbohydrate; 25 g protein; 1 g fiber; 134 mg sodium; 573 mg potassium.

Nutrition Bonus: Selenium (60% daily value), Vitamin C (25% dv), Magnesium (24% dv), Potassium (16% dv).

Healthy)(Weight

Lower ⬇ Carbs

- **1**   **tablespoon lemon juice**
- **1**   **tablespoon extra-virgin olive oil**
- **½**   **teaspoon minced garlic**
     Freshly ground pepper to taste
- **8**   **ounces Pacific halibut *or* mahi-mahi, cut into 2 portions**
- **1**   **tablespoon sesame seeds, toasted (*see Tip, page 245*)**
- **1**   **teaspoon dried thyme leaves**
- **⅛**   **teaspoon coarse sea salt *or* kosher salt**
     Lemon wedges

1. Preheat oven to 450°F. Line a baking sheet with foil.

2. Mix lemon juice, oil, garlic and pepper in a shallow glass dish. Add fish and turn to coat. Cover and marinate in the refrigerator for 15 minutes.

3. Meanwhile, combine sesame seeds and thyme in a small bowl.

4. Sprinkle the fish with salt and coat evenly with the sesame seed mixture, covering the sides as well as the top. Transfer the fish to the prepared baking sheet and roast until just cooked through, 10 to 14 minutes. Serve with lemon wedges.

MAKES **2** SERVINGS.

Pacific Sole with Oranges & Pecans

Active Minutes: **20**

Total: **20 minutes**

Per Serving: 234 calories; 9 g
fat (3 g sat, 3 g mono); 70 mg
cholesterol; 11 g carbohydrate;
28 g protein; 2 g fiber; 401 mg
sodium; 556 mg potassium.

Nutrition Bonus: Vitamin C
(70% daily value), Calcium
(20% dv), Selenium (16% dv).

Healthy)(Weight

Lower ⬇ Carbs

Ingredient Note:

● The term "sole" is widely
used for many types of flatfish from both the Atlantic
and Pacific. Flounder and
Atlantic halibut are included
in the group that is often
identified as "sole" or "grey
sole." The best choices are
Pacific, Dover, English or
Petrale sole. Other sole and
flounder are overfished.

Dover sole, swimming in butter, once graced the table of every restaurant serving "Continental cuisine." But sole is more versatile than
that: with just a little effort (and some thoughtful shopping; *see Note*)
it becomes a satisfying, healthy, one-skillet dinner.

1	seedless orange
10	ounces Pacific sole (*see Note*) *or* tilapia fillets
¼	teaspoon salt
¼	teaspoon freshly ground pepper
2	teaspoons unsalted butter
1	medium shallot, minced
2	tablespoons white-wine vinegar
2	tablespoons chopped pecans, toasted (*see Tip, page 245*)
2	tablespoons chopped fresh dill

1. Using a sharp paring knife, remove the skin and white pith from orange.
Hold the fruit over a small bowl and cut between the membranes to
release individual orange sections into the bowl, collecting any juice as well (See
tip, page 244). Discard membranes, pith and skin.

2. Sprinkle both sides of fish with salt and pepper. Coat a large nonstick
skillet with cooking spray and place over medium heat. Add the fish and
cook 1 minute for sole or 3 minutes for tilapia. Gently flip and cook until the
fish is opaque in the center and just cooked through, 1 to 2 minutes for sole or
3 to 5 minutes for tilapia. Divide between 2 serving plates; cover with foil to
keep warm.

3. Add butter to the pan and melt over medium heat. Add shallot and cook,
stirring, until soft, about 30 seconds. Add vinegar and the orange sections
and juice; loosen any browned bits on the bottom of the pan and cook for
30 seconds. Spoon the sauce over the fish and sprinkle each portion with pecans
and dill. Serve immediately.

MAKES **2** SERVINGS.

Mediterranean Fish Fillets

This is "pan-Mediterranean" in its flavors and employs a method of cooking fish by keeping it moist in a zesty sauce. You can also add capers, roasted peppers or sun-dried tomatoes to the sauce.

1   **teaspoon extra-virgin olive oil**
1   **small onion, thinly sliced**
2   **tablespoons dry white wine**
1   **clove garlic, finely chopped**
1   **cup canned diced tomatoes (*see Tips for Two*)**
4   **Kalamata olives, pitted (*see Tip, page 245*) and chopped**
1/8 **teaspoon dried oregano**
1/8 **teaspoon freshly grated orange zest**
1/4 **teaspoon salt, divided**
1/4 **teaspoon freshly ground pepper, divided**
8   **ounces thick-cut, firm-fleshed fish fillets, such as Pacific halibut *or* mahi-mahi**

1. Preheat oven to 450°F.

2. Heat oil in a medium nonstick skillet over medium-high heat. Add onion and cook, stirring often, until lightly browned, 2 to 4 minutes. Add wine and garlic and simmer for 30 seconds. Stir in tomatoes, olives, oregano and orange zest. Season with 1/8 teaspoon salt and 1/8 teaspoon pepper.

3. Season fish with the remaining 1/8 teaspoon each salt and pepper. Arrange the fish in a single layer in a pie pan or baking dish. Spoon the tomato mixture over the fish. Bake, uncovered, until the fish is just cooked through, 10 to 20 minutes. Divide the fish into 2 portions and serve with sauce.

MAKES **2** SERVINGS.

Active Minutes: **30**

Total: **45 minutes**

Per Serving: **222 calories; 7 g fat (1 g sat, 4 g mono); 36 mg cholesterol; 9 g carbohydrate; 25 g protein; 2 g fiber; 766 mg sodium; 579 mg potassium.**

Nutrition Bonus: **Selenium (60% daily value), Vitamin C (30% dv), Magnesium (25% dv), Potassium (17% dv).**

Healthy Weight

Lower Carbs

Tips for Two
CANNED DICED TOMATOES
STORAGE: Refrigerate up to 1 week, freeze for up to 3 months.
USES: Add to soups and salsa; use to bulk up marinara sauce; add to an omelet with sliced green onions and shredded pepper Jack cheese.

Salt & Pepper Shrimp

Rice flour is the "secret ingredient" in this dish and is used to make the flavorful coating for the shrimp. But if you can't find it, cornstarch makes a fine substitute. Serve with rice noodles or brown rice and a sprinkle of chopped scallions.

- **2   tablespoons lime juice**
- **2   teaspoons reduced-sodium soy sauce**
- **2   teaspoons toasted sesame oil**
- **1/2   teaspoon sugar**
- **3   cups thinly sliced cabbage, preferably napa (about 1/4 head; see Tips for Two, page 248)**
- **1   small red or orange bell pepper, very thinly sliced**
- **2   tablespoons rice flour (see Note) or cornstarch**
- **1/4   teaspoon kosher salt**
- **1/2   teaspoon freshly ground pepper**
- **1/2   teaspoon five-spice powder (see Note, page 246)**
- **10   ounces raw shrimp (21-25 per pound), peeled and deveined**
- **1   tablespoon canola oil**
- **1   jalapeño or serrano pepper, seeded and minced**

1. Whisk lime juice, soy sauce, sesame oil and sugar in a large bowl until the sugar is dissolved. Add cabbage and bell pepper; toss to combine.

2. Combine rice flour (or cornstarch), salt, pepper and five-spice powder in a medium bowl. Add shrimp and toss to coat. Heat oil in a large nonstick skillet over medium-high heat. Add the shrimp and cook, stirring often, until they are pink and curled, 3 to 4 minutes. Add jalapeño (or serrano) and cook until the shrimp are cooked through, about 1 minute more. Serve the slaw topped with the shrimp.

MAKES **2** SERVINGS.

Active Minutes: **30**

Total: 30 minutes

Per Serving: 347 calories; 15 g fat (2 g sat, 7 g mono); 230 mg cholesterol; 20 g carbohydrate; 34 g protein; 3 g fiber; 558 mg sodium; 408 mg potassium.

Nutrition Bonus: Vitamin C (190% daily value), Selenium (83% dv), Vitamin A (60% dv), Iron (25% dv).

Healthy)(Weight

Lower ↓ Carbs

Ingredient Note:

- Rice flour is made from finely milled white rice. It is often used in Asian cooking for desserts and to thicken sauces. Look for it in Asian markets or the natural-foods section of your supermarket.

Seared Scallops with Grapefruit Sauce

G rapefruit juice and segments, combined with honey, make a thick and flavorful sauce. Serve with broccoli sprinkled with toasted pine nuts and a crisp rosé to round out the meal.

Active Minutes: **35**

Total: **40 minutes**

Per Serving: **258** calories; **8 g** fat (1 g sat, 4 g mono); **37 mg** cholesterol; **23 g** carbohydrate; **20 g** protein; **1 g** fiber; **257 mg** sodium; **589 mg** potassium.

Nutrition Bonus: **Vitamin C (70% daily value), Vitamin A (25% dv), Magnesium (20% dv), Potassium (17% dv).**

Healthy)(Weight

- **1 small pink grapefruit**
- **8 ounces dry sea scallops (*see Note, page 247*)**
- **1/8 teaspoon kosher salt**
- **1/8 teaspoon freshly ground pepper**
- **3 teaspoons canola oil, divided**
- **1 shallot, thinly sliced**
- **2 tablespoons dry vermouth *or* dry white wine**
- **1 tablespoon honey**
- **1 tablespoon chopped fresh mint**

1. Remove skin and white pith from grapefruit using a sharp knife and discard. Hold the fruit over a bowl and cut between the membrane to release individual sections into the bowl, collecting the juice as well (*see photo, page 244*). Squeeze any remaining juice from the membranes into the bowl. Discard the seeds and membranes. Drain the juice into a measuring cup and add water, if necessary, to make 1/4 cup.

2. Sprinkle both sides of scallops with salt and pepper. Heat 2 teaspoons oil in a medium nonstick skillet over medium-high heat. Add the scallops and cook until golden, 3 to 4 minutes per side. Transfer the scallops to a plate and cover with foil to keep warm.

3. Add the remaining 1 teaspoon oil to the pan. Add shallot and cook, stirring often, until softened, about 1 minute. Add the reserved grapefruit juice and vermouth (or wine) and bring to a boil. Boil until reduced by half, about 3 minutes. Reduce heat to low and add honey, the grapefruit sections and mint. Return the scallops to the pan and reheat gently, turning to coat with the sauce.

MAKES **2** SERVINGS.

Barbecued Mussels

A take-off on New Orleans "barbecued" shrimp (also made on the stovetop), this combines shellfish with a piquant barbecue sauce that will have you licking your fingers. A 2-pound bag of mussels is just the right amount for serving a pair.

- 2 teaspoons peanut oil *or* canola oil
- 1 large red onion, finely chopped
- 2 cloves garlic, minced
- 1 tablespoon paprika
- 1 tablespoon dry mustard
- 1 tablespoon chili powder
- ½ teaspoon freshly ground pepper
- ½ cup tomato sauce (*see Tips for Two, page 248*)
- 2 tablespoons cider vinegar
- 2 teaspoons Worcestershire sauce
- 1 teaspoon liquid smoke (optional)
- 1½ teaspoons honey
  Hot sauce, such as Tabasco, to taste
- 2 pounds mussels, scrubbed and debearded (*see Tip*)

1. Heat oil in a large saucepan over medium heat. Add onion and garlic. Cook, stirring frequently, until softened, 6 to 8 minutes. Stir in paprika, dry mustard, chili powder and pepper. Cook, stirring, until fragrant, about 30 seconds. Pour in tomato sauce, vinegar, Worcestershire sauce, liquid smoke (if using), honey and hot sauce, stirring to scrape up any browned bits. Bring to a simmer. Add mussels and stir to combine. Return to a simmer. Cover, reduce heat and simmer until the mussels open, 6 to 8 minutes. Stir; discard any unopened mussels before serving.

MAKES 2 SERVINGS.

Active Minutes: **35**

Total: 40 minutes

Per Serving: 316 calories; 11 g fat (2 g sat, 3 g mono); 48 mg cholesterol; 31 g carbohydrate; 24 g protein; 5 g fiber; 793 mg sodium; 776 mg potassium.

Nutrition Bonus: Vitamin A (80% daily value), Iron (60% dv), Vitamin C (45% dv), Folate & Potassium (22% dv).

Healthy ⧓ Weight

High ⬆ Fiber

Tip:

- To debeard a mussel, hold it in one hand and firmly pull out the black fibrous "beard" from the shell (*see photo, page 244*).

Saffron-Scented Mussels

When you think "mussels" you may not instantly think "chickpeas," but the two are joined in tasteful union in this delicious, bistro-style dish. You'll want some crusty bread to sop up the sauce.

Active Minutes: **35**

Total: **40 minutes**

Per Serving: 371 calories; 10 g fat (2 g sat, 5 g mono); 48 mg cholesterol; 39 g carbohydrate; 27 g protein; 7 g fiber; 619 mg sodium; 729 mg potassium.

Nutrition Bonus: Vitamin C (130% daily value), Vitamin A (50% dv), Iron (45% dv), Folate (36% dv), Potassium (21% dv).

High ⬆ Fiber

2   **teaspoons extra-virgin olive oil**
1   **8-ounce can chickpeas, rinsed**
8   **cherry tomatoes, halved**
1   **small onion, chopped**
2   **cloves garlic, minced**
1   **4-ounce jar chopped pimientos, rinsed**
2   **teaspoons chopped fresh oregano**
½   **teaspoon freshly ground pepper**
    Pinch of saffron
½   **cup vegetable broth *or* reduced-sodium chicken broth (*see Tips for Two, page 248*)**
¼   **cup dry sherry (*see Note, page 247*)**
2   **pounds mussels, scrubbed and debearded (*see Tip, page 244*)**

I Heat oil in a large saucepan over medium heat. Add chickpeas, tomatoes, onion, garlic and pimientos. Cook, stirring frequently, until softened, 6 to 8 minutes. Stir in oregano, pepper and saffron. Cook, stirring, until fragrant, about 30 seconds. Pour in broth and sherry, stirring to scrape up any browned bits. Bring to a simmer. Add mussels and stir to combine. Return to a simmer. Cover, reduce heat and simmer until the mussels open, 6 to 8 minutes. Stir; discard any unopened mussels before serving.

MAKES **2** SERVINGS.

CHAPTER 6

Beef, Pork & Lamb

Grilled Rib-eye Steak with Tomato Salad & Chimichurri

I n Argentina, chimichurri—a spicy herb sauce—is a standard condiment, and almost always accompanies *asado* (grilled meat). Serve with warm bread and a Malbec wine.

Active Minutes: **30**

Total: 30 minutes

Per Serving: 343 calories; 18 g fat (4 g sat, 11 g mono); 69 mg cholesterol; 9 g carbohydrate; 36 g protein; 2 g fiber; 369 mg sodium; 861 mg potassium.

Nutrition Bonus: Vitamin C (60% daily value), Zinc (47% dv), Vitamin A (45% dv), Potassium (25% dv).

Healthy)(Weight

Lower ⬇ Carbs

Chimichurri (*page 225*)

Salad

2	medium tomatoes, cut into wedges
¼	cup thinly sliced sweet onion
2	teaspoons extra-virgin olive oil
2	teaspoons distilled white vinegar
⅛	teaspoon kosher salt
⅛	teaspoon freshly ground pepper

Steak

8	ounces boneless rib-eye steak, about 1-inch thick, trimmed of fat, cut into 2 portions
½	teaspoon extra-virgin olive oil
⅛	teaspoon kosher salt
⅛	teaspoon freshly ground pepper

1. ♦ Prepare Chimichurri. Preheat the grill to high.

2. ♦ **To prepare salad:** Combine tomatoes, onion, oil and vinegar in a medium bowl. Season with salt and pepper.

3. ♦ **To prepare steak:** Rub steak with oil. Season on both sides with salt and pepper. Grill the steak 3 to 4 minutes per side for medium-rare. Allow the steak to rest for 5 minutes; serve with the salad on the side and a dollop of Chimichurri on top.

MAKES **2** SERVINGS.

Coffee Bean & Peppercorn Steak

Here's a recipe that packs a wallop. The bold combination of coffee beans and peppercorns works well on other rich meats, such as venison. Serve with Beet Bliss (*page 227*) and a glass of Cabernet.

Active Minutes: **25**

Total: 25 minutes

Per Serving: 190 calories; 8 g fat (3 g sat, 4 g mono); 55 mg cholesterol; 2 g carbohydrate; 25 g protein; 0 g fiber; 195 mg sodium; 347 mg potassium.

Nutrition Bonus: Selenium (39% daily value), Zinc (33% dv).

Healthy ⚖ Weight

Lower ⬇ Carbs

1	**small clove garlic**
1/4	**teaspoon kosher salt, divided**
1	**tablespoon strong freshly brewed coffee**
1	**tablespoon balsamic vinegar**
	Freshly ground pepper to taste
1	**tablespoon whole coffee beans (not flavored beans)**
1	**teaspoon whole black peppercorns**
1/2	**teaspoon extra-virgin olive oil**
8	**ounces sirloin steak, about 1 inch thick, trimmed of fat**

1. Preheat grill to high.

2. Smash and peel garlic clove, sprinkle with 1/8 teaspoon salt and mash into a paste with a spoon or the side of a chef's knife. Transfer to a small bowl and whisk in coffee and vinegar. Season with pepper.

3. Place coffee beans and peppercorns on a cutting board; coarsely crush with the bottom of a heavy pan. Mix the crushed coffee beans and peppercorns together. Rub steaks with oil, sprinkle with the remaining 1/8 teaspoon salt and coat with the coffee-peppercorn mixture, pressing it into the meat. Grill 4 to 5 minutes per side for medium rare.

4. Transfer the steak to a cutting board and let rest 5 minutes. Thinly slice across the grain. Serve with the vinaigrette.

MAKES **2** SERVINGS.

Marrakech Grilled Steak & Sweet Potatoes

Filling a packet of foil with vegetables to cook on the grill is one of our favorite techniques. Here it results in tender, steaming sweet potatoes and onions with a hint of the grill and, best of all, no pans to wash!

- ½ **teaspoon ground allspice**
- ½ **teaspoon ground cumin**
- ½ **teaspoon ground ginger**
- ½ **teaspoon kosher salt**
- ¼ **teaspoon ground cinnamon**
- ¼ **teaspoon ground coriander**
- ¼ **teaspoon cayenne pepper**
- 8 **ounces strip steak, trimmed of fat and cut into 2 portions**
- 1 **medium sweet potato, peeled and very thinly sliced**
- 1 **small red onion, halved and very thinly sliced**
- 2 **teaspoons canola oil**
- ½ **teaspoon freshly grated orange zest**

1. Preheat grill to high.

2. Combine allspice, cumin, ginger, salt, cinnamon, coriander and cayenne in a medium bowl. Sprinkle steaks with 2¼ teaspoons of the spice mixture. Add sweet potato and onion to the bowl along with oil and zest; toss to coat.

3. Place two 24-inch sheets of foil on top of each other (the double layers will help protect the ingredients from burning). Generously coat the top piece with cooking spray. Spread the sweet potato mixture in the center of the foil in a thin layer. Bring the short ends of foil together, fold over and pinch to seal. Pinch the seams together along the sides to seal the packet.

4. Place the packet on the hottest part of the grill and cook, turning once, about 5 minutes per side. Cook the steaks, turning once, 3 to 4 minutes per side for medium-rare. Transfer to plates and let rest while the packet finishes cooking. Open the packet (be careful of steam) and serve alongside the steaks.

MAKES **2** SERVINGS.

Active Minutes: **30**

Total: 30 minutes

Per Serving: 366 calories; 15 g fat (4 g sat, 7 g mono); 78 mg cholesterol; 21 g carbohydrate; 34 g protein; 3 g fiber; 369 mg sodium; 621 mg potassium.

Nutrition Bonus: Vitamin A (220% daily value), Zinc (40% dv), Vitamin C (20% dv), Iron (15% dv).

Lower ⬇ Carbs

Chili-Rubbed Steaks & Pan Salsa

Any cut of steak will work for this recipe, but we especially like the flavor and texture of rib-eye with these seasonings; look for steak that has been thinly cut. A cold ale, warm tortillas and Vinegary Coleslaw (*page 227*) can round out the meal.

Active Minutes: **20**

Total: 20 minutes

Per Serving: 174 calories; 9 g fat (3 g sat, 4 g mono); 60 mg cholesterol; 4 g carbohydrate; 20 g protein; 1 g fiber; 336 mg sodium; 421 mg potassium.

Nutrition Bonus: Zinc (27% daily value), Vitamin A (20% dv), Vitamin C (15% dv).

Healthy ✕ Weight

Lower ⬇ Carbs

8 ounces ½-inch-thick steaks, such as rib-eye, trimmed of fat and cut into 2 portions
1 teaspoon chili powder
½ teaspoon kosher salt, divided
1 teaspoon extra-virgin olive oil
2 plum tomatoes, diced
2 teaspoons lime juice
1 tablespoon chopped fresh cilantro

1. Sprinkle both sides of steak with chili powder and ¼ teaspoon salt. Heat oil in a medium skillet over medium-high heat. Add the steaks and cook, turning once, 1 to 2 minutes per side for medium-rare. Transfer the steaks to a plate, cover with foil and let rest while you make the salsa.

2. Add tomatoes, lime juice and the remaining ¼ teaspoon salt to the pan and cook, stirring often, until the tomatoes soften, about 3 minutes. Remove from heat, stir in cilantro and any accumulated juices from the steaks. Serve the steaks topped with the salsa.

MAKES **2** SERVINGS.

Herb-Coated Filet Mignon

I t doesn't get much easier than this. If you can turn on your broiler, chop some herbs and open a jar of mustard then you have a simple and elegant dish. Turn it into a meal by adding sautéed spinach and half a baked potato with reduced-fat sour cream and prepared horseradish.

- **8 ounces filet mignon, about 2 inches thick, trimmed of fat and cut into 2 portions**
- **1 teaspoon extra-virgin olive oil**
- **⅛ teaspoon kosher salt**
- **⅛ teaspoon freshly ground pepper**
- **2 tablespoons chopped mixed fresh herbs, such as chives, parsley, chervil, tarragon *and/or* thyme**
- **1 teaspoon Dijon mustard**

1. ◆ Preheat broiler.

2. ◆ Rub steaks with oil; sprinkle with salt and pepper. Place on a rack on a broiler pan.

3. ◆ Broil until an instant-read thermometer inserted into the steak registers 140°F for medium-rare, 15 to 20 minutes total, turning once halfway through cooking. Transfer to a cutting board; let rest for 5 minutes.

4. ◆ Place herbs on a plate. Coat the edges of the steaks evenly with mustard; then roll the edges in the herbs, pressing gently to adhere.

MAKES **2** SERVINGS.

Active Minutes: **10**

Total: **25 minutes**

Per Serving: **222 calories; 13 g fat (4 g sat, 6 g mono); 75 mg cholesterol; 1 g carbohydrate; 25 g protein; 0 g fiber; 184 mg sodium; 328 mg potassium.**

Nutrition Bonus: **Selenium (39% daily value), Zinc (33% dv).**

Healthy ⟩⟨ Weight

Lower ⬇ Carbs

Grilled Steak with Beets & Radicchio

Peppery radicchio mellows a bit on the grill and is offset wonderfully by the sweet beets and earthy goat cheese dressing. Simple and superb. Rib-eye or filet would also be a delicious choice in this recipe.

- **2 tablespoons crumbled goat cheese *or* feta cheese**
- **2 teaspoons white-wine vinegar *or* champagne vinegar**
- **¼ teaspoon dry mustard**
- **1 tablespoon minced shallot**
- **2 teaspoons minced fresh parsley**
- **¼ teaspoon kosher salt, divided**
- **¼ teaspoon freshly ground pepper, divided**
- **3½ teaspoons extra-virgin olive oil, divided**
- **1 small head radicchio, halved, cored and each half quartered**
- **1 8-ounce can baby beets, drained**
- **8 ounces New York strip (loin) steak, trimmed of fat and cut into 2 portions**

Active Minutes: **30**

Total: 30 minutes

Per Serving: 320 calories; 17 g fat (5 g sat, 10 g mono); 57 mg cholesterol; 15 g carbohydrate; 26 g protein; 3 g fiber; 456 mg sodium; 801 mg potassium.

Nutrition Bonus: Zinc (33% daily value), Folate (28% dv), Iron & Vitamin C (25% dv), Potassium (23% dv).

Healthy)(Weight

Lower ⬇ Carbs

1. Preheat grill to high.

2. Place cheese in a medium bowl and mash it with the back of a spoon until creamy. Add vinegar, dry mustard, shallot, parsley, ⅛ teaspoon salt and ⅛ teaspoon pepper; whisk to combine. Slowly drizzle in 2 teaspoons oil and whisk until blended.

3. Thread radicchio chunks and beets onto skewers and drizzle with 1 teaspoon oil. Rub steaks with the remaining ½ teaspoon oil. Season the steaks and skewered vegetables with the remaining ⅛ teaspoon salt and pepper.

4. Grill the steaks 3 to 4 minutes per side for medium-rare. Grill the vegetable skewers, turning frequently, until the radicchio is wilted and lightly charred, 5 to 7 minutes. Transfer the steaks to a plate; let rest for 5 minutes. Remove the vegetables from the skewers. Serve steaks and vegetables with the sauce.

MAKES **2** SERVINGS.

Korean Beef Stir-Fry

Inspired by the flavors found in Korean barbecue, this dish is a mouth-watering addition to any weeknight repertoire. A fruity Riesling and rice noodles are perfect accompaniments.

Active Minutes: **30**

Total: 30 minutes

Per Serving: 399 calories; 17 g fat (4 g sat, 8 g mono); 45 mg cholesterol; 28 g carbohydrate; 33 g protein; 6 g fiber; 660 mg sodium; 1,125 mg potassium.

Nutrition Bonus: Vitamin A (160% daily value), Vitamin C (90% dv), Folate (75% dv), Iron (35% dv), Potassium (32% dv).

High ⬆ Fiber

Tip:

- If you have a little extra time before dinner, put the steak in the freezer for about 20 minutes to help make it easier to slice thinly.

3 tablespoons mirin (*see Note, page 246*)
2 tablespoons reduced-sodium soy sauce
2 teaspoons cornstarch
1 tablespoon canola oil
8 ounces flank steak, trimmed of fat and very thinly sliced against the grain (*see Tip*)
1 tablespoon chopped garlic
2 teaspoons chopped jalapeño pepper, or to taste
1½ teaspoons chopped fresh ginger
4 cups mung bean sprouts
1 6-ounce bag baby spinach
¼ cup chopped fresh cilantro
1 teaspoon toasted sesame oil
2 tablespoons toasted sesame seeds (*see Tip, page 245*), optional

1. Combine mirin, soy sauce and cornstarch in a small bowl.

2. Heat oil in a large nonstick skillet over medium-high heat. Spread steak out in the pan and cook until seared on one side, about 1 minute. Add garlic, jalapeño and ginger and cook, stirring, until fragrant, about 30 seconds. Add bean sprouts and spinach (the pan will be very full). Pour the mirin mixture into the pan and stir gently until the sauce thickens and the spinach is wilted, about 3 minutes. Stir in cilantro and sesame oil. Serve topped with sesame seeds (if using).

MAKES 2 SERVINGS, 2 CUPS EACH.

Fennel-Crusted Sirloin Tips with Bell Peppers

The mild anise flavor of fennel seed is balanced by the rich-tasting pan gravy and peppers. Serve with egg noodles tossed with parsley and a drizzle of extra-virgin olive oil.

Active Minutes: **35**

Total: **35 minutes**

Per Serving: 327 calories; 15 g fat (4 g sat, 9 g mono); 55 mg cholesterol; 13 g carbohydrate; 28 g protein; 3 g fiber; 364 mg sodium; 719 mg potassium.

Nutrition Bonus: Vitamin C (380% daily value), Vitamin A (70% dv), Zinc (33% dv), Potassium (21% dv).

Healthy ⊁ **Weight**

Lower ⬇ **Carbs**

8	ounces sirloin steak, trimmed of fat and cut into 1-inch chunks
1	teaspoon fennel seed, roughly chopped *or* coarsely ground in a spice mill
1/2	teaspoon kosher salt, divided
1	tablespoon extra-virgin olive oil
1	tablespoon minced garlic
3/4	cup reduced-sodium beef broth, divided (*see Tips for Two, page 248*)
1/4	cup dry red wine
2	bell peppers, cut into 1-inch squares
	Freshly ground pepper to taste
1	tablespoon all-purpose flour

1. Rub steak with fennel seed and 1/4 teaspoon salt, turning to coat on all sides. Heat oil in a large skillet over medium-high heat. Add the steak in a single layer and cook, turning once, until browned on the outside and still pink in the middle, 2 to 4 minutes. Transfer to a plate and cover with foil to keep warm.

2. Add garlic to the pan and cook, stirring constantly, until fragrant, about 30 seconds. Add 1/2 cup broth and wine, scraping up any browned bits with a wooden spoon. Add bell peppers, the remaining 1/4 teaspoon salt and pepper; bring to a simmer. Cover, reduce heat to maintain a simmer and cook until the peppers are tender-crisp, 4 to 6 minutes.

3. Whisk the remaining 1/4 cup broth and flour in a small bowl. Add to the pepper mixture, increase heat to medium-high and bring to a simmer, stirring constantly. Return the steak to the pan. Adjust heat to maintain a slow simmer and cook, turning the meat once, about 2 minutes for medium-rare.

MAKES **2** SERVINGS.

Burgers with Caramelized Onions

A h, the magic of seared beef! Sautéing the onions with sugar turns them into a meltingly sweet topping to dress up these hearty beef-and-bulgur patties.

3 **tablespoons bulgur**
1/4 **cup boiling water plus 2 tablespoons water, divided**
2 **teaspoons extra-virgin olive oil**
2 **cups sliced onions**
1 **teaspoon sugar**
1 **teaspoon balsamic vinegar**
1/4 **teaspoon salt, divided**
8 **ounces 92%-lean ground beef**
1 **tablespoon tomato paste (*see Tips for Two*)**
2 **tablespoons chopped fresh parsley**
1/4 **teaspoon freshly ground pepper**
2 **whole-wheat hamburger buns, split and toasted**
   Lettuce for garnish

Active Minutes: **30**

Total: 40 minutes

Per Serving: 403 calories; 15 g fat (5 g sat, 8 g mono); 72 mg cholesterol; 38 g carbohydrate; 30 g protein; 7 g fiber; 644 mg sodium; 714 mg potassium.

Nutrition Bonus: Zinc (47% daily value), Iron (25% dv), Magnesium (23% dv), Potassium (20% dv), Vitamin A & Vitamin C (15% dv).

High ⬆ Fiber

1. Combine bulgur and 1/4 cup boiling water in a small bowl; let stand until most of the water is absorbed, 20 to 30 minutes.

2. Meanwhile, heat oil in a nonstick skillet over medium-low heat. Add onions and sugar; cook, stirring occasionally, until the onions are very tender and golden, about 15 minutes. Stir in 2 tablespoons water, vinegar and 1/8 teaspoon salt. Keep warm over very low heat, stirring occasionally.

3. Preheat the grill or broiler to high. Combine the bulgur, beef, tomato paste, parsley, the remaining 1/8 teaspoon salt and pepper in a medium bowl; knead thoroughly to combine. Shape into two 3/4-inch-thick patties. Grill or broil on a lightly oiled rack until browned and cooked through, about 5 minutes per side. Place the patties on buns, top with the caramelized onions and garnish with lettuce.

MAKES **2** SERVINGS.

Tips for Two
TOMATO PASTE
STORAGE: Transfer to an airtight container and refrigerate for up to 1 week or freeze for up to 3 months. USES: Add to soups, chilis and sauces; stir into rice with oregano and cilantro to serve alongside Mexican dishes.

Asian Salisbury Steaks

Back in the 19th century, an English doctor named J.H. Salisbury prescribed beef for all manner of ailments. We think he'd love this healthy update of the ground-beef-and-onions classic that bears his name. The sautéed watercress is an excellent foil to the meaty glazed beef.

6	ounces 90%-lean ground beef
1/3	cup finely diced red bell pepper
1/3	cup chopped scallions
2	tablespoons plain dry breadcrumbs
2	tablespoons hoisin sauce, divided
1	tablespoon minced fresh ginger
1½	teaspoons canola oil, divided
8	cups trimmed watercress (2 bunches *or* one 4-ounce bag)
1/4	cup Shao Hsing rice wine *or* dry sherry (*see Note, page 247*)

Active Minutes: **25**

Total: **30 minutes**

Per Serving: **302 calories; 13 g fat (4 g sat, 6 g mono); 56 mg cholesterol; 17 g carbohydrate; 21 g protein; 2 g fiber; 391 mg sodium; 611 mg potassium.**

Nutrition Bonus: **Vitamin C (120% daily value), Vitamin A (70% dv), Zinc (27% dv), Potassium (17% dv).**

Healthy)(**Weight**

Lower ⬇ **Carbs**

1. Place rack in upper third of oven; preheat the broiler. Coat a broiler pan and rack with cooking spray.

2. Gently mix beef, bell pepper, scallions, breadcrumbs, 1 tablespoon hoisin sauce and ginger in a medium bowl until just combined. Form the mixture into 2 oblong patties and place on the prepared broiler-pan rack. Brush the tops of the patties with ½ teaspoon oil. Broil, flipping once, until cooked through, about 4 minutes per side.

3. Meanwhile, heat the remaining 1 teaspoon oil in a large skillet over high heat. Add watercress and cook, stirring often, until just wilted, 1 to 3 minutes. Divide the watercress between 2 plates. Return the pan to medium-high heat. Add rice wine (or sherry) and the remaining 1 tablespoon hoisin sauce. Cook, stirring, until smooth, bubbling and slightly reduced, about 1 minute. Top the watercress with the Salisbury steaks and drizzle with the pan sauce.

MAKES **2** SERVINGS.

Cube Steak Milanese

Grated sharp Italian cheese in the breading for the cube steaks is echoed in the salad—using shavings instead. The addition of the green salad makes for a well-balanced dinner.

Active Minutes: **25**

Total: 25 minutes

Per Serving: 398 calories; 21 g fat (6 g sat, 8 g mono); 141 mg cholesterol; 15 g carbohydrate; 36 g protein; 2 g fiber; 704 mg sodium; 329 mg potassium.

Nutrition Bonus: Vitamin C (32% daily value), Vitamin A (30% dv), Calcium & Iron (25% dv).

Lower ⬇ Carbs

- **2** plum tomatoes, seeded and chopped
- **1/4** cup diced red onion
- **1/4** teaspoon salt, divided
- **1** large egg
- **1/4** cup plain dry breadcrumbs
- **2** tablespoons grated Pecorino Romano *or* Parmesan cheese plus 2 tablespoons shaved (*see Tip, page 245*), divided
- **1** tablespoon minced fresh parsley (optional)
- **8** ounces cube steak, cut into 2 portions
- **1/4** teaspoon freshly ground pepper, divided
- **4** teaspoons extra-virgin olive oil, divided
- **2** cups baby arugula *or* spinach, chopped
- **1/3** cup thinly sliced fresh basil leaves
- **2** teaspoons lemon juice, plus lemon wedges for garnish

1. Combine tomato, onion and 1/8 teaspoon salt in a large bowl. Set aside to allow the tomatoes to release their juices.

2. Whisk egg in a shallow dish. Combine breadcrumbs, grated cheese and parsley (if using) in another dish. Season steak with the remaining 1/8 teaspoon salt and 1/8 teaspoon pepper. Dip each piece into the egg, allowing excess to drip off, then dredge in the breadcrumb mixture.

3. Heat 1 teaspoon oil in a medium nonstick skillet over medium heat. Add the steaks and cook until golden brown on the first side, 2 to 3 minutes. Turn the steaks over, add 1 teaspoon oil and cook until the steaks are cooked through, 3 to 4 minutes more. Transfer to a plate; cover with foil to keep warm.

4. Add shaved cheese, the remaining 1/8 teaspoon pepper, the remaining 2 teaspoons oil, arugula (or spinach), basil and lemon juice to the tomato mixture; toss to combine. Serve the steaks on a bed of the arugula-tomato salad. Garnish with lemon wedges.

MAKES **2** SERVINGS.

Pork Chops with Maple-Mustard Sauce

As Vermonters, we think a touch of maple syrup makes anything better, and these chops are proof. Round out the meal with Wild Rice Salad (*page 228*), roasted delicata squash and a glass of Pinot Noir.

1½   teaspoons plus 1 tablespoon Dijon mustard, divided
¼   teaspoon kosher salt
¼   teaspoon freshly ground pepper
2   boneless pork loin chops (8 ounces), trimmed of fat
1   teaspoon canola oil
¼   cup cider vinegar
2   tablespoons maple syrup
1½   teaspoons chopped fresh sage *or* ½ teaspoon rubbed dried sage

Active Minutes: **25**

Total: 25 minutes

Per Serving: 254 calories; 10 g fat (3 g sat, 5 g mono); 65 mg cholesterol; 15 g carbohydrate; 25 g protein; 0 g fiber; 475 mg sodium; 382 mg potassium.

Nutrition Bonus: Selenium (53% daily value), Zinc (20% dv).

Healthy)(Weight

Lower ⬇ Carbs

1. Combine 1½ teaspoons mustard, salt and pepper in a small bowl. Rub all over pork.

2. Heat oil in a medium skillet over medium-high heat. Add the pork and cook until browned on both sides and cooked through, 2 to 3 minutes per side. Transfer to a cutting board and cover with foil.

3. While the pork is resting, heat vinegar in the skillet over medium-high heat. Boil, scraping up any browned bits with a wooden spoon, about 30 seconds. Whisk in the remaining 1 tablespoon mustard and maple syrup. Bring to a boil, reduce heat to a simmer and cook until the sauce is thickened, about 3 minutes. Add any accumulated juices from the pork to the sauce, along with sage. Serve the pork topped with the sauce.

MAKES **2** SERVINGS.

Pork Cutlets with Cumberland Sauce

Old-fashioned, sweet and sour Cumberland Sauce, a British favorite, makes a fine topping for pork. Round out the meal with roasted new potatoes and sautéed greens.

Active Minutes: **15**

Total: **15 minutes**

Per Serving: 270 calories; 9 g fat (3 g sat, 5 g mono); 65 mg cholesterol; 11 g carbohydrate; 24 g protein; 0 g fiber; 208 mg sodium; 422 mg potassium.

Nutrition Bonus: Selenium (54% daily value).

Healthy)(Weight

Lower ⬇ Carbs

1	**teaspoon extra-virgin olive oil**
2	**thin-cut boneless pork chops (8 ounces), trimmed of fat**
¼	**teaspoon kosher salt**
¼	**teaspoon freshly ground pepper**
1	**small shallot, minced**
½	**cup dry red wine**
½	**teaspoon cornstarch**
1 ½	**teaspoons red-wine vinegar**
1	**tablespoon red currant jelly**
½	**teaspoon brown sugar (optional)**
½	**teaspoon Dijon mustard**

1. Heat oil in a medium skillet over medium-high heat. Season pork with salt and pepper, transfer to the pan and cook until browned and no longer pink in the middle, 1 to 2 minutes per side. Transfer to a plate and cover with foil to keep warm.

2. Add shallot to the pan and cook, stirring constantly, until softened, 30 seconds to 1 minute. Add wine and bring to a boil, stirring constantly. Boil until reduced to about 2 tablespoons, 2 to 3 minutes. Whisk cornstarch and vinegar in a small bowl; whisk into the sauce. Cook, stirring, until thickened and glossy, about 30 seconds. Remove from the heat and stir in jelly, sugar (if using), mustard and any accumulated juices from the pork. Serve the pork with the sauce.

MAKES **2** SERVINGS.

Cider Vinegar-&-Molasses-Glazed Pork Chops

Serve these chops, dripping with sauce, on whole-wheat rolls for a Southern-style sandwich, or serve on a plate with some coleslaw and beans. A tall glass of minty iced tea will balance out the tangy sauce.

- **1 teaspoon extra-virgin olive oil**
- **2 thin-cut boneless pork chops (8 ounces), trimmed of fat**
- **1 shallot, finely chopped**
- **½ jalapeño pepper, seeded and finely chopped**
- **1 clove garlic, finely chopped**
- **2 tablespoons molasses**
- **2 tablespoons cider vinegar**
- **1 tablespoon Dijon mustard**
- **1 teaspoon reduced-sodium soy sauce**

1. Heat oil over medium-high heat in a medium skillet. Add pork, and cook until browned and no longer pink in the middle, 1 to 2 minutes per side. Transfer to a plate and cover with foil to keep warm.

2. Add shallot, jalapeño and garlic; cook, stirring often, until slightly softened, 2 to 3 minutes. Add molasses, vinegar, mustard and soy sauce and bring to a simmer. Reduce heat to maintain a simmer and cook, stirring occasionally, until thickened, 2 to 4 minutes. Return the pork and any accumulated juices to the pan and turn to coat with sauce. Serve the pork with the sauce.

MAKES **2** SERVINGS.

Active Minutes: **20**

Total: 20 minutes

Per Serving: 262 calories; 9 g fat (3 g sat, 5 g mono); 65 mg cholesterol; 20 g carbohydrate; 25 g protein; 0 g fiber; 245 mg sodium; 693 mg potassium.

Nutrition Bonus: Selenium (60% daily value), Potassium (20% dv), Magnesium (19% dv).

Healthy ⫡ Weight

Lower ⬇ Carbs

BEEF, PORK & LAMB

Pork with Dried Apples & Prosciutto

Our favorite fall flavors come together in this simple skillet supper, united in a tangy cider sauce. Accompany the pork with mashed potatoes—perfect for soaking up the sauce.

Active Minutes: **30**

Total: 30 minutes

Per Serving: 369 calories; 11 g fat (3 g sat, 5 g mono); 77 mg cholesterol; 39 g carbohydrate; 30 g protein; 3 g fiber; 663 mg sodium; 454 mg potassium.

Nutrition Bonus: Selenium (54% daily value).

- 2   thin-cut boneless pork loin chops (8 ounces), trimmed of fat
- 1/8   teaspoon kosher salt, or to taste
- 1/8   teaspoon freshly ground pepper
- 1   teaspoon extra-virgin olive oil
- 2   thin slices prosciutto (1 ounce), chopped
- 1   cup apple cider
- 3/4   cup chopped dried apples
- 1/2   cup reduced-sodium chicken broth, divided (*see Tips for Two, page 248*)
- 1   teaspoon cider vinegar
- 1   teaspoon chopped fresh sage *or* 1/4 teaspoon rubbed dried sage
- 2   teaspoons whole-grain mustard
- 1   teaspoon cornstarch

1. Sprinkle pork chops with salt and pepper. Heat oil in a large nonstick skillet over medium-high heat. Add the pork and cook until browned on both sides, 1 to 2 minutes per side. Transfer to a plate. Add prosciutto and cook, stirring constantly, until browned, about 1 minute. Transfer to the plate.

2. Add cider, apples, 1/4 cup broth, vinegar and sage to the pan, increase heat to medium-high and bring to a boil, scraping up any browned bits. Reduce heat to a simmer and cook, stirring occasionally, until the apples have softened, 4 to 6 minutes.

3. Stir together mustard, cornstarch and the remaining 1/4 cup broth in a small bowl. Add to the pan and bring to a simmer, stirring constantly. Return the pork and prosciutto to the pan and simmer, turning the pork to coat, until heated through, 1 to 2 minutes.

MAKES **2** SERVINGS.

Marjoram-Rubbed Pork & Grilled Potato Salad

Summery and full of fresh herb flavors, this dish is as colorful as it is tasty. If you have fresh summer squash or eggplant, grill it as well and toss it into the salad. Serve with a green salad and cold lemonade.

- **1 small clove garlic, minced**
- **2 tablespoons extra-virgin olive oil**
- **2 tablespoons minced fresh marjoram *or* oregano**
- **¼ teaspoon salt, or to taste**
- **¼ teaspoon freshly ground pepper**
- **2 boneless pork loin chops (8 ounces), trimmed of fat**
- **3 tablespoons red-wine vinegar**
- **6 small red potatoes, halved**
- **1 small red bell pepper, cut into 2-inch chunks**
- **1 small red onion, cut into 1½-inch chunks**
- **¼ cup crumbled feta cheese**
- **6 green olives, pitted and chopped**

1. Preheat grill to high.

2. Combine garlic, oil, marjoram (or oregano), salt and pepper in a medium bowl. Rub 1 teaspoon of the mixture into both sides of pork. Transfer 1 tablespoon of the mixture to a large bowl and whisk in vinegar until combined. Add potatoes, bell pepper and onion to the medium bowl; toss to coat.

3. Oil the grill rack (*see Tip*). Reduce heat to medium and grill the potatoes, turning often, until tender, 15 to 20 minutes. Thread the onion and pepper chunks onto two 10-inch skewers. Grill, turning often, until charred in spots and tender, 10 to 15 minutes. Grill the pork, turning once, 6 to 8 minutes total.

4. Add the grilled vegetables to the bowl with the reserved dressing along with feta and olives; toss to coat. Serve the pork with the salad.

MAKES **2** SERVINGS.

Active Minutes: **45**

Total: **45 minutes**

Per Serving: 480 calories; 26 g fat (7 g sat, 16 g mono); 77 mg cholesterol; 31 g carbohydrate; 30 g protein; 4 g fiber; 583 mg sodium; 1,127 mg potassium.

Nutrition Bonus: Vitamin C (170% daily value), Selenium (59% dv), Vitamin A (25% dv), Zinc (20% dv).

Tip:

- To oil a grill rack, oil a folded paper towel, hold it with tongs and rub it over the rack. (Do not use cooking spray on a hot grill.)

Pork Tenderloin with Gingered Mango Sauce

A vibrant mango sauce—also great with chicken or fish—will have you dreaming of warm and balmy Key West. Serve it with brown basmati rice and a salad of mixed greens.

Active Minutes: **25**

Total: 30 minutes

Per Serving: 273 calories; 7 g fat (2 g sat, 3 g mono); 63 mg cholesterol; 30 g carbohydrate; 23 g protein; 2 g fiber; 328 mg sodium; 528 mg potassium.

Nutrition Bonus: Selenium (56% daily value), Vitamin C (50% dv), Potassium (15% dv).

Healthy ⑂ Weight

8	ounces pork tenderloin (*see Tips for Two*), trimmed of fat
1/2	teaspoon chopped fresh rosemary
1/2	teaspoon chopped fresh thyme
1/2	teaspoon kosher salt, divided
1/2	teaspoon freshly ground pepper, divided
1	teaspoon extra-virgin olive oil
2	tablespoons brown sugar
1	tablespoon red-wine vinegar
1	tablespoon dry sherry (*see Note, page 247*)
2	teaspoons finely chopped fresh ginger
1	medium mango, peeled and diced

Tips for Two
PORK TENDERLOIN
STORAGE: Tightly wrap unused portion and freeze for up to 6 months.
USES: Dice and add to soups; add strips to stir-fries; sauté with potatoes and onions for a quick hash.

1. ◆ Preheat oven to 400°F.

2. ◆ Rub pork with rosemary, thyme, ¼ teaspoon salt and ¼ teaspoon pepper. Heat oil in a medium ovenproof skillet over medium-high heat; add the pork and cook, turning occasionally, until browned on all sides, about 4 minutes. Transfer the pan to the oven and roast until an instant-read thermometer inserted into the center of the pork registers 145°F for medium, 12 to 15 minutes. Transfer the pork to a cutting board and let rest 5 minutes.

3. ◆ Return the pan to medium-high heat. (Use caution because the handle will still be very hot.) Add sugar, vinegar, sherry and ginger; cook, stirring constantly, until the sugar is melted, about 1 minute. Stir in mango and remove from the heat. Transfer the mixture to a blender or food processor. Puree until smooth. Slice the pork and serve with the sauce.

MAKES **2** SERVINGS.

Pork & Red Pepper Hash

R ed bell pepper and scallions add crunch and color to this full-flavored hash. Steak, chicken or turkey could be substituted for the pork, if you like.

1   tablespoon all-purpose flour
1   boneless pork loin chop (4 ounces), trimmed of fat and cut into ½-inch pieces
4   teaspoons extra-virgin olive oil, divided
1   small onion, diced
2   cups frozen diced hash brown potatoes
1   small red bell pepper, diced
½   teaspoon hot *or* sweet paprika
½   teaspoon garlic powder
½   teaspoon chopped fresh rosemary
½   teaspoon salt
    Freshly ground pepper to taste
2   scallions, sliced
1   teaspoon cider vinegar

Active Minutes: **20**

Total: 20 minutes

Per Serving: 391 calories; 14 g fat (3 g sat, 9 g mono); 32 mg cholesterol; 49 g carbohydrate; 18 g protein; 5 g fiber; 365 mg sodium; 934 mg potassium.

Nutrition Bonus: Vitamin C (150% daily value), Vitamin A (30% dv), Potassium (27% dv).

High ⬆ Fiber

1. Sprinkle flour over pork and turn to coat both sides. Heat 2 teaspoons oil in a large nonstick skillet over medium-high heat. Spread the pork evenly in the pan and cook until lightly browned on one side, 1 to 2 minutes. Continue cooking, stirring occasionally, until evenly browned, 1 to 2 minutes more. Transfer the pork to a plate and cover with foil to keep warm.

2. Heat the remaining 2 teaspoons oil in the pan over medium-high heat. Add onion and cook, stirring often, until starting to brown, 1 to 3 minutes. Add potatoes, bell pepper, paprika, garlic powder, rosemary, salt and pepper. Cook, stirring frequently, until the potatoes are browned and crispy in spots, 4 to 8 minutes. Add the pork and scallions and cook, stirring often, until the pork is heated through, about 2 minutes. Stir in vinegar.

MAKES 2 SERVINGS, ABOUT 1 ½ CUPS EACH.

Penne with Vodka Sauce & Capicola

Just when did vodka sauce for pasta become so popular? We don't know, but we approve; especially when it's given a nutritional makeover. For an extra serving of vegetables, stir in some cooked fresh or frozen peas at the end.

Active Minutes: 20

Total: 30 minutes

To Make Ahead: Cover and refrigerate the sauce for up to 3 days.

Per Serving: 330 calories; 2 g fat (0 g sat, 0 g mono); 7 mg cholesterol; 55 g carbohydrate; 13 g protein; 7 g fiber; 563 mg sodium; 178 mg potassium.

Nutrition Bonus: Iron & Vitamin A (20% daily value), Vitamin C (15% dv).

High ↑ Fiber

Ingredient Note:

● Capicola and pancetta are flavorful cured Italian meats. Capicola tends to be more spicy and pancetta more salty; both are used to enhance flavors in Italian cooking. Buy one thick piece from the supermarket deli for this recipe.

4	**ounces whole-wheat penne**
1	**1-ounce piece capicola *or* pancetta, finely diced (*see Note*)**
1	**large shallot, chopped**
1	**clove garlic, chopped**
¼	**cup vodka**
1	**8-ounce can no-salt-added tomato sauce**
⅛	**teaspoon salt, or to taste**
2	**tablespoons half-and-half *or* whole milk (optional)**
1	**teaspoon Worcestershire sauce**
⅛	**teaspoon crushed red pepper, or to taste**
2	**tablespoons chopped fresh basil**
	Freshly ground pepper to taste

1. Bring a large pot of water to a boil. Cook penne until just tender, 12 minutes or according to package directions.

2. Meanwhile, cook capicola (or pancetta) in a small saucepan over medium heat until crisp, about 4 minutes. Transfer with a slotted spoon to a paper-towel lined plate.

3. Return the pot to medium-low heat; add shallot and garlic to the drippings and cook until fragrant and beginning to soften, about 1 minute. Increase heat to high; add vodka and bring to a boil. Boil until reduced by about half, about 1 minute. Stir in tomato sauce, salt, half-and-half (or milk), if using, Worcestershire sauce and crushed red pepper to taste. Reduce to a simmer and cook until thickened, about 5 minutes.

4. Drain the pasta; serve topped with the sauce and sprinkled with the capicola (or pancetta), basil and pepper.

MAKES **2** SERVINGS.

Sausage & Lentil Casserole

Requiring 45 minutes from start to finish, this casserole classic is one of the longer recipes in this book; however, it takes only about 10 minutes to assemble. While it bakes, you can put together a salad, or simply enjoy a glass of wine. If you want to make it vegetarian, substitute soy "sausage" for the Italian sausage and vegetable broth for the chicken broth.

Active Minutes: **10**

Total: **45 minutes**

Per Serving: 467 calories; 13 g fat (5 g sat, 2 g mono); 42 mg cholesterol; 58 g carbohydrate; 29 g protein; 18 g fiber; 748 mg sodium; 93 mg potassium.

Nutrition Bonus: Vitamin A (200% daily value), Folate (61% dv), Iron (33% dv), Potassium (17% dv).

High ⬆ Fiber

1 teaspoon extra-virgin olive oil
1 link hot Italian sausage, casing removed
1 small onion, chopped
1 14-ounce can lentils, rinsed
1 cup cooked frozen *or* fresh spinach
¾ cup reduced-sodium chicken broth (*see Tips for Two, page 248*)
1 teaspoon dried oregano
¾ cup instant brown rice
⅛ teaspoon freshly ground pepper
¼ cup shredded extra-sharp Cheddar cheese

1. Preheat oven to 400°F. Coat a 1-quart casserole or loaf pan with cooking spray.

2. Heat oil in a medium skillet over medium heat. Add sausage and onion; cook, stirring, until the onion softens, about 5 minutes. Add lentils, spinach, broth and oregano. Increase heat to medium-high and cook, stirring often, until heated through, about 3 minutes. Stir in rice and pepper. Transfer the mixture to the prepared baking dish and cover with foil. Bake until the rice is tender, 30 to 35 minutes. Top with cheese and bake, uncovered, until the cheese melts, about 2 minutes more.

MAKES **2** SERVINGS.

Migas with Chorizo

Migas—a dish of eggs scrambled with torn-up corn tortillas—was created as a way to use up stale tortillas. So if you have some sitting around, use those and skip the toasting instructions in Step 1.

4 corn tortillas, cut into 1-by-2-inch strips

2 large eggs

4 large egg whites

2 tablespoons prepared tomato salsa

1 teaspoon canola oil

¼ cup chopped onion

1 jalapeño pepper, seeded and minced

¼ cup finely diced chorizo (*see Note*)

1 medium tomato, diced

¼ cup shredded reduced-fat Cheddar cheese

1. Preheat oven to 400°F. Place tortilla strips on a baking sheet and bake until lightly crisped, about 5 minutes.

2. Whisk eggs, egg whites and salsa in a medium bowl. Heat oil in a large nonstick skillet over medium heat. Add onion, jalapeño, chorizo and the toasted tortillas; cook, stirring frequently, until the onion is softened, 2 to 3 minutes. Add the egg mixture, reduce heat to medium-low and cook, stirring occasionally, until the eggs are set, about 2 minutes. Add tomato and cook, stirring, until heated through, about 1 minute. Remove from the heat and stir in cheese.

MAKES **2** SERVINGS, 1 **1/2** CUPS EACH.

Active Minutes: **20**

Total: 20 minutes

Per Serving: 375 calories; 18 g fat (6 g sat, 8 g mono); 233 mg cholesterol; 31 g carbohydrate; 22 g protein; 5 g fiber; 560 mg sodium; 560 mg potassium.

Nutrition Bonus: Vitamin C (25% daily value), Vitamin A (20% dv), Calcium & Iron (15% dv).

High ⬆ Fiber

Ingredient Note:

● Chorizo, a spicy pork sausage seasoned with paprika and chili, is originally from Spain and is often used in Mexican cooking. Chorizo can be made with raw or smoked, ground or chopped pork. Chorizo is available at well-stocked supermarkets, specialty food stores or online at tienda.com.

Lamb Chops with Mint Pan Sauce

Instead of serving lamb with plain old mint jelly, whip up this simple yet impressive pan sauce. Serve with asparagus and wild rice or quick-cooking barley (*see page 239*) and peas cooked with fresh mint.

1/4 **cup apple juice**

3/4 **teaspoon cornstarch**

4 **lamb loin chops (12 ounces), trimmed of fat**

1/4 **teaspoon kosher salt**

1/4 **teaspoon freshly ground pepper**

1 **teaspoon canola oil**

1 **small shallot, minced**

1/4 **cup reduced-sodium beef broth (*see Tips for Two, page 248*)**

1 **tablespoon cider vinegar**

1 **tablespoon mint jelly**

1 **tablespoon minced fresh mint, divided**

1. Preheat oven to 450°F. Combine apple juice and cornstarch in a small bowl. Set aside.

2. Sprinkle lamb chops with salt and pepper. Heat oil in a large ovenproof skillet over medium-high heat. Add the chops and cook until browned on one side, about 2 minutes. Turn them over and transfer the pan to the oven. Roast until an instant-read thermometer inserted horizontally into a chop registers 140°F for medium-rare, 6 to 10 minutes, depending on the thickness. Transfer the chops to a plate and cover with foil to keep warm.

3. Place the pan over medium-high heat. (Be careful, the handle will still be hot.) Add shallot and cook, stirring constantly, until browned and softened, about 1 minute. Add broth, vinegar and jelly; bring to a boil, whisking to dissolve the jelly. Cook, whisking constantly, until the liquid has reduced by half, 2 to 3 minutes. Stir the cornstarch mixture; add it to the pan. Bring to a simmer and cook, stirring, until the sauce has thickened, about 30 seconds. Remove from the heat and stir in half the mint along with any accumulated juices from the lamb. Serve the chops topped with the sauce and the remaining mint.

MAKES **2** SERVINGS.

Active Minutes: **35**

Total: 40 minutes

Per Serving: 227 calories; 9 g fat (3 g sat, 4 g mono); 68 mg cholesterol; 12 g carbohydrate; 22 g protein; 0 g fiber; 259 mg sodium; 341 mg potassium.

Nutrition Bonus: Selenium (34% daily value), Zinc (20% dv).

Healthy ✕ Weight

Lower ⬇ Carbs

BEEF, PORK & LAMB

Orzo with Lamb, Olives & Feta

Sure, orzo is good in soup, but there's no need to stop there. Here it's a base for a bold blend of spices, tomato sauce and flavorful ground lamb. The optional pinch of crushed red pepper will add the heat that many crave.

Active Minutes: **30**

Total: 30 minutes

Per Serving: 452 calories; 17 g fat (6 g sat, 7 g mono); 46 mg cholesterol; 56 g carbohydrate; 21 g protein; 4 g fiber; 403 mg sodium; 699 mg potassium.

Nutrition Bonus: Vitamin C (30% daily value), Vitamin A (25% dv), Potassium & Zinc (20% dv).

½ **cup orzo**

4 **ounces lean ground lamb *or* ground beef *or* ground turkey**

2 **teaspoons extra-virgin olive oil**

1 **small onion, finely chopped**

1 **clove garlic, minced**

¼ **teaspoon ground cinnamon**

¼ **teaspoon crumbled dried rosemary *or* oregano**
Pinch of crushed red pepper (optional)

1 **8-ounce can no-salt-added tomato sauce**

1 **tablespoon pitted, chopped black olives**

⅛ **teaspoon salt**

⅛ **teaspoon freshly ground pepper, or to taste**

2 **tablespoons crumbled feta cheese**

1. Bring a large saucepan of water to a boil. Cook orzo until just tender, about 8 minutes or according to package directions. Drain.

2. Meanwhile, cook lamb (or beef or turkey) in a medium nonstick skillet over medium heat, stirring, until browned, 2 to 3 minutes. Drain in a sieve set over a bowl. Clean and dry the pan.

3. Add oil to the pan and heat over medium heat. Add onion and cook, stirring, until softened, 3 to 5 minutes. Add garlic, cinnamon, rosemary (or oregano) and crushed red pepper (if using); cook, stirring, until fragrant, about 1 minute. Add the lamb (or beef or turkey) and tomato sauce; cook, stirring occasionally, until the sauce is thickened, 5 to 7 minutes. Remove from the heat and stir in olives, salt and pepper. Toss the orzo with the sauce. Serve garnished with feta.

MAKES **2** SERVINGS, **1** CUP EACH.

Lamb Kafta Pockets

These Middle Eastern-style meatballs are best wrapped in a warm pita pocket, with plenty of shredded lettuce and slivered red onion and, of course, some of the sweet-and-tangy sauce.

Apricot Sauce

- **6 dried apricots**
- **⅓ cup orange juice**
- **2 tablespoons chopped fresh mint**
- **2 tablespoons water**
- **1 teaspoon red-wine vinegar**

Lamb Kafta

- **⅓ cup whole-wheat couscous**
- **⅓ cup boiling water**
- **4 ounces ground lamb**
- **1 tablespoon chopped fresh parsley**
- **1 teaspoon minced garlic**
- **¼ teaspoon salt**
- **⅛ teaspoon ground allspice**
- **1 teaspoon extra-virgin olive oil**
- **2 whole-wheat pitas, sliced open on top and toasted**

Active Minutes: **40**

Total: 40 minutes

To Make Ahead: The sauce can be made up to 1 day in advance.

Per Serving: 439 calories; 12 g fat (4 g sat, 5 g mono); 37 mg cholesterol; 67 g carbohydrate; 19 g protein; 10 g fiber; 566 mg sodium; 644 mg potassium.

Nutrition Bonus: Vitamin C (40% daily value), Vitamin A (30% dv), Iron (20% dv).

High 🡁 Fiber

1. **To prepare apricot sauce:** Combine apricots and orange juice in a small microwave-safe bowl and microwave on High until bubbling, about 1 minute. Set aside to soften for 10 minutes. Transfer the apricot mixture to a food processor or blender. Add mint, water and vinegar; puree until smooth.

2. **To prepare lamb kafta:** Place couscous in a medium bowl. Pour boiling water over it and let stand until the water is absorbed, about 5 minutes. Add lamb, parsley, garlic, salt and allspice to the couscous and knead until the mixture is sticky and holds together. Form into 6 balls of equal size.

3. Heat oil in a medium nonstick skillet. Add the meatballs and cook, turning often to prevent scorching, until browned on all sides, about 6 minutes. Pour ½ cup water into the skillet, cover and cook until the meatballs are cooked through, about 4 minutes. Using a slotted spoon, transfer the meatballs to a plate. Serve the meatballs inside pitas topped with the apricot sauce.

MAKES **2** SERVINGS.

Accompaniments

Quick Sauces

Avocado-Grapefruit Relish

With a sharp knife, remove the peel and white pith from 1 large seedless grapefruit and discard. Cut the grapefruit segments from the surrounding membrane, letting them drop into a bowl (*see photo, page 244*). Add ½ diced avocado, 1 small minced shallot, 1 tablespoon chopped fresh cilantro and 1 teaspoon each red-wine vinegar and honey. Toss well to combine.

MAKES 3/4 CUP.

Per Tablespoon: 24 calories; 1 g fat (0 g sat, 1 g mono); 0 mg cholesterol; 3 g carbohydrate; 0 g protein; 1 g fiber; 1 mg sodium; 80 mg potassium.

Buttermilk Ranch Dressing

Whisk ¼ cup buttermilk, 2 tablespoons reduced-fat mayonnaise, 1 tablespoon champagne (*or white-wine*) vinegar and ¼ teaspoon each garlic powder, salt and freshly ground pepper in a small bowl until smooth. Stir in 2 tablespoons chopped fresh herbs, such as chives, tarragon, basil *or* dill.

MAKES 1/2 CUP.

Per Tablespoon: 16 calories; 1 g fat (0 g sat, 0 g mono); 1 mg cholesterol; 1 g carbohydrate; 0 g protein; 0 g fiber; 103 mg sodium; 17 mg potassium.

Caesar Salad Dressing

Put ½ small clove garlic and ⅛ teaspoon salt in a medium bowl and mash with the back of a spoon to form a paste. Add 2 tablespoons lemon juice, 1 tablespoon reduced-fat mayonnaise, 1 teaspoon Dijon mustard, ¾ teaspoon anchovy paste, or to taste (optional), and ¼ teaspoon freshly ground pepper; whisk to combine. Slowly drizzle in 4 teaspoons extra-virgin olive oil, whisking constantly. Add 2 tablespoons grated Asiago cheese and whisk to combine.

MAKES ABOUT 1/2 CUP.

Per Tablespoon: 32 calories; 3 g fat (1 g sat, 2 g mono); 2 mg cholesterol; 1 g carbohydrate; 0 g protein; 0 g fiber; 78 mg sodium; 5 mg potassium.

Chimichurri

Chop ½ cup packed fresh parsley and 1 teaspoon chopped garlic together on a cutting board until the parsley is finely minced. Transfer to a medium bowl, add 5 teaspoons distilled white vinegar, 2 teaspoons extra-virgin olive oil, ¼ teaspoon kosher salt and ⅛ teaspoon ground chipotle (*or cayenne*) pepper; stir to combine.

MAKES 1/4 CUP.

Per Tablespoon: 26 calories; 2 g fat (0 g sat, 2 g mono); 0 mg cholesterol; 1 g carbohydrate; 0 g protein; 0 g fiber; 74 mg sodium; 46 mg potassium.

Cilantro-Lime Vinaigrette

Puree ½ cup packed fresh cilantro, ¼ cup extra-virgin olive oil, 2 tablespoons each lime juice and orange juice, ¼ teaspoon each salt and freshly ground pepper and a pinch of minced garlic in a blender or food processor until smooth.

MAKES ABOUT 2/3 CUP.

Per Tablespoon: 53 calories; 6 g fat (1 g sat, 4 g mono); 0 mg cholesterol; 1 g carbohydrate; 0 g protein; 0 g fiber; 59 mg sodium; 14 mg potassium.

Buttermilk Ranch Dressing

Cilantro-Lime Vinaigrette

Maple-Mustard Vinaigrette

Creamy Dill Sauce

Combine 2 tablespoons reduced-fat mayonnaise, 2 table-spoons nonfat plain yogurt, 1 thinly sliced scallion, 1½ teaspoons lemon juice, 1½ teaspoons finely chopped fresh dill (*or* parsley) and freshly ground pepper to taste in a small bowl.

MAKES ABOUT ¼ CUP.

Per Tablespoon: 28 calories; 2 g fat (0 g sat, 0 g mono); 2 mg cholesterol; 2 g carbohydrate; 0 g protein; 0 g fiber; 50 mg sodium.

Cucumber-Dill Raita

Combine ½ cup nonfat plain yogurt, ½ small diced cucumber and 1 tablespoon chopped fresh dill in a small bowl. Season with salt and freshly ground pepper to taste. Cover and chill until ready to serve.

MAKES ABOUT ½ CUP.

Per Tablespoon: 8 calories; 0 g fat (0 g sat, 0 g mono); 0 mg cholesterol; 1 g carbohydrate; 1 g protein; 0 g fiber; 27 mg sodium; 14 mg potassium.

Maple-Mustard Sauce

Combine ¼ cup whole-grain mustard and 2 tablespoons maple syrup in a small bowl.

MAKES ⅓ CUP.

Per Tablespoon: 35 calories; 1 g fat (0 g sat, 0 g mono); 0 mg cholesterol; 7 g carbohydrate; 1 g protein; 0 g fiber; 232 mg sodium; 36 mg potassium.

Maple-Mustard Vinaigrette

Whisk ¼ cup walnut (*or* canola) oil, 2 tablespoons each maple syrup and cider vinegar, 1 tablespoon each coarse-grained mustard and reduced-sodium soy sauce and ¼ teaspoon each salt and freshly ground pepper in a small bowl.

MAKES ABOUT ⅔ CUP.

Per Tablespoon: 62 calories; 6 g fat (1 g sat, 1 g mono); 0 mg cholesterol; 3 g carbohydrate; 0 g protein; 0 g fiber; 143 mg sodium; 16 mg potassium.

Spicy Plum Chutney

Pit and chop 1 large plum (about ¼ pound). Place in a small saucepan; add 2 teaspoons red-wine vinegar, 2 teaspoons honey and a pinch of crushed red pepper, or to taste. Bring to a simmer over high heat, stirring often. Cover, reduce heat, and simmer, stirring occasionally, until the plum starts to break down. Transfer to a blender or food processor and pulse several times into a coarse puree.
MAKES ⅓ CUP.

Per Tablespoon: 48 calories; 0 g fat (0 g sat, 0 g mono); 0 mg cholesterol; 12 g carbohydrate; 0 g protein; 1 g fiber; 0 mg sodium; 94 mg potassium.

Tomato & Avocado Salsa

Combine 1 large diced tomato, ¼ cup diced red onion, ½ minced jalapeño, 2 to 3 tablespoons lime juice, ¼ teaspoon kosher salt and ⅛ teaspoon freshly ground pepper in a medium bowl. Stir in ½ diced avocado and ¼ cup chopped fresh cilantro. Taste and add a pinch of cayenne if you want some extra spice.
MAKES ABOUT 1½ CUPS.

Per Tablespoon: 9 calories; 1 g fat (0 g sat, 0 g mono); 0 mg cholesterol; 1 g carbohydrate; 0 g protein; 0 g fiber; 13 mg sodium; 44 mg potassium.

Quick Sides

EACH RECIPE MAKES 2 SERVINGS.

SALADS

Beet Bliss

Toss 2 cups baby spinach with ½ cup quartered cooked beets, 1 tablespoon chopped toasted pecans and 2 tablespoons crumbled goat cheese. Serve with Maple-Mustard Vinaigrette (*page 226*).

Per Serving: 155 calories; 11 g fat (3 g sat, 3 g mono); 7 mg cholesterol; 11 g carbohydrate; 4 g protein; 2 g fiber; 266 mg sodium; 165 mg potassium.

Lemony Carrot Salad

Whisk 1 tablespoon each lemon juice and extra-virgin olive oil, ½ small minced garlic clove, ⅛ teaspoon salt and freshly ground pepper to taste in a medium bowl. Add 1 cup grated carrots, 1½ tablespoons chopped fresh dill and 1 tablespoon chopped scallion; toss to coat.

Per Serving: 90 calories; 7 g fat (1 g sat, 5 g mono); 0 mg cholesterol; 6 g carbohydrate; 1 g protein; 2 g fiber; 184 mg sodium; 198 mg potassium.

Orange & Avocado Salad

Toss 2 cups crisp greens with 1 segmented orange, ½ chopped avocado and 2 tablespoons slivered red onion. Serve with Cilantro-Lime Vinaigrette (*page 225*).

Per Serving: 167 calories; 13 g fat (2 g sat, 9 g mono); 0 mg cholesterol; 13 g carbohydrate; 2 g protein; 6 g fiber; 76 mg sodium; 524 mg potassium.

Vinegary Coleslaw

Whisk 2 tablespoons white-wine vinegar, 1 tablespoon canola oil, 1 teaspoon each sugar and Dijon mustard, and a pinch each of celery seed and salt in a medium bowl. Add 1½ cups shredded cabbage, 1 grated carrot and ¼ cup slivered red onion and toss to coat.

Per Serving: 101 calories; 7 g fat (1 g sat, 4 g mono); 0 mg cholesterol; 9 g carbohydrate; 1 g protein; 2 g fiber; 138 mg sodium; 248 mg potassium.

Warm Apple-Cabbage Slaw

Place 1½ cups shredded cabbage, 1 thinly sliced apple and ¼ cup apple juice (*or broth or water*) in a medium skillet, cover and cook until tender. Stir in cider vinegar and salt to taste.

Per Serving: 68 calories; 0 g fat (0 g sat, 0 g mono); 0 mg cholesterol; 18 g carbohydrate; 1 g protein; 4 g fiber; 156 mg sodium; 168 mg potassium.

The Wedge

Cut 1 heart of romaine lengthwise into quarters; remove core. Top with 1 tablespoon chopped chives, 1 slice crumbled, cooked bacon and 2 tablespoons crumbled blue cheese. Serve the salad with Buttermilk Ranch Dressing (*page 225*).

Per Serving: 70 calories; 5 g fat (2 g sat, 1 g mono); 11 mg cholesterol; 3 g carbohydrate; 4 g protein; 1 g fiber; 297 mg sodium; 61 mg potassium.

Wild Rice Salad

Stir 2 tablespoons chopped dried fruit, 1 tablespoon each chopped toasted nuts and orange juice and 1 teaspoon extra-virgin olive oil into 1 cup cooked wild rice (*see page 239*).

Per Serving: 153 calories; 5 g fat (1 g sat, 3 g mono); 0 mg cholesterol; 24 g carbohydrate; 4 g protein; 2 g fiber; 3 mg sodium; 208 mg potassium.

GRAINS

Asian Brown Rice

Cook brown rice (*see page 239*), adding 1 teaspoon minced fresh ginger to the cooking liquid. Stir ½ diced red bell pepper, ¼ cup chopped water chestnuts and a splash each of reduced-sodium soy sauce and toasted sesame oil into the cooked rice.

Per Serving: 130 calories; 2 g fat (0 g sat, 1 g mono); 0 mg cholesterol; 27 g carbohydrate; 3 g protein; 3 g fiber; 26 mg sodium; 145 mg potassium.

Herbed Whole-Wheat Couscous

Bring ¾ cup reduced-sodium chicken broth, 2 sliced scallions and 2 tablespoons chopped fresh parsley to a boil in a small saucepan. Add ½ cup whole-wheat couscous, return to a simmer, cover and remove from the heat. Let stand, covered, 5 minutes. Fluff with a fork before serving.

Per Serving: 256 calories; 1 g fat (0 g sat, 0 g mono); 2 mg cholesterol; 47 g carbohydrate; 10 g protein; 8 g fiber; 57 mg sodium; 62 mg potassium.

Polenta-Asiago Croutons

Cube ½ tube of polenta. Sauté the polenta cubes in 1 teaspoon extra-virgin olive oil in a nonstick skillet until golden. Remove from the heat, sprinkle with 3 tablespoons shredded Asiago cheese, cover and let stand until the cheese melts. Sprinkle with cracked black pepper.

Per Serving: 152 calories; 6 g fat (2 g sat, 2 g mono); 9 mg cholesterol; 20 g carbohydrate; 5 g protein; 2 g fiber; 497 mg sodium; 0 mg potassium.

Provençal Barley

Toss 1 cup cooked barley (*see page 239*) with 1 chopped plum tomato, 2 chopped pitted Kalamata olives and ¼ teaspoon herbes de Provence.

Per Serving: 115 calories; 1 g fat (0 g sat, 1 g mono); 0 mg cholesterol; 24 g carbohydrate; 2 g protein; 4 g fiber; 65 mg sodium; 157 mg potassium.

Quick Cheese Grits

Combine 1½ cups water, 6 tablespoons quick-cooking grits and a pinch each of salt and garlic powder in a small saucepan. Bring to a boil, stirring constantly. Reduce to a simmer, cover and cook, stirring occasionally, until desired consistency. Remove from the heat and stir in ¼ cup shredded sharp Cheddar cheese and a pinch of paprika, stirring until the cheese melts.

Per Serving: 153 calories; 5 g fat (3 g sat, 0 g mono); 15 mg cholesterol; 23 g carbohydrate; 6 g protein; 1 g fiber; 166 mg sodium; 25 mg potassium.

Quinoa & Black Beans

Sauté ½ chopped bell pepper and 2 tablespoons chopped red onion in 1 teaspoon canola oil until almost tender. Add ½ cup rinsed canned black beans and 2 tablespoons broth (*or* water) to the pan. Cook until heated through. Stir in ½ cup hot cooked quinoa (*see page 239*).

Per Serving: 162 calories; 4 g fat (0 g sat, 2 g mono); 0 mg cholesterol; 27 g carbohydrate; 6 g protein; 4 g fiber; 60 mg sodium; 224 mg potassium.

Orange & Avocado Salad

BREAD & POTATOES

Buttermilk-Herb Mashed Potatoes

Peel 1 large Yukon Gold potato and cut into chunks. Place in a small saucepan and cover with water. Add 1 peeled garlic clove. Bring to a boil; cook until the potato is tender. Drain; add 1 teaspoon butter and 2 tablespoons nonfat buttermilk, and mash with a potato masher to the desired consistency. Stir in 1½ teaspoons chopped fresh herbs. Season with salt and freshly ground pepper.

Per Serving: 85 calories; 2 g fat (1 g sat, 0 g mono); 5 mg cholesterol; 14 g carbohydrate; 2 g protein; 1 g fiber; 87 mg sodium; 416 mg potassium.

Garlic-Tomato Toasts

Grill or toast 2 slices whole-wheat country bread. Cut a small garlic clove and small plum tomato in half. Rub one side of the toasted bread with the cut-side of a garlic clove half and drizzle with extra-virgin olive oil. Rub with the cut-side of a tomato half. Sprinkle with kosher salt and coarsely ground pepper.

Per Serving: 91 calories; 4 g fat (1 g sat, 2 g mono); 0 mg cholesterol; 13 g carbohydrate; 3 g protein; 2 g fiber; 183 mg sodium; 82 mg potassium.

Garlic-Tomato Toasts

Oven Fries

Preheat oven to 450°F. Cut 1 large Yukon Gold potato into wedges. Toss with 2 teaspoons extra-virgin olive oil, ¼ teaspoon salt and ¼ teaspoon dried thyme (optional).

Oven Fries

Avocado-Corn Salsa

Lemon Lovers' Asparagus

Mary's Zucchini with Parmesan

Spread the wedges out on a rimmed baking sheet. Bake until browned and tender, turning once, about 20 minutes total.

Per Serving: 103 calories; 5 g fat (1 g sat, 4 g mono); 0 mg cholesterol; 13 g carbohydrate; 2 g protein; 1 g fiber; 291 mg sodium; 407 mg potassium.

Oven Sweet Potato Fries

Preheat oven to 450°F. Peel 1 large sweet potato and cut into wedges. Toss with 2 teaspoons canola oil, ¼ teaspoon salt and a pinch of cayenne pepper. Spread the wedges out on a rimmed baking sheet. Bake until browned and tender, turning once, about 20 minutes total.

Per Serving: 122 calories; 5 g fat (0 g sat, 3 g mono); 0 mg cholesterol; 19 g carbohydrate; 2 g protein; 3 g fiber; 323 mg sodium; 429 mg potassium.

VEGETABLES

Avocado-Corn Salsa

Combine ½ diced avocado, ½ cup thawed frozen corn kernels, 1 chopped plum tomato and 2 teaspoons chopped fresh cilantro in a small bowl. Add lime juice and salt to taste.

Per Serving: 105 calories; 8 g fat (1 g sat, 0 g mono); 0 mg cholesterol; 12 g carbohydrate; 3 g protein; 3 g fiber; 76 mg sodium; 364 mg potassium.

Lemon Lovers' Asparagus

Preheat oven to 450°F. Trim 1 bunch of asparagus and thinly slice 1 lemon. Toss on a rimmed baking sheet with 1 tablespoon extra-virgin olive oil, 2 teaspoons chopped fresh oregano and ¼ teaspoon each salt and freshly ground pepper. Roast, shaking the pan occasionally, until the asparagus is tender-crisp, 10 to 15 minutes.

Per Serving: 91 calories; 7 g fat (1 g sat, 5 g mono); 0 mg cholesterol; 9 g carbohydrate; 2 g protein; 4 g fiber; 302 mg sodium; 241 mg potassium.

Orange-Infused Green Beans & Red Pepper

Mary's Zucchini with Parmesan

Heat 1 teaspoon extra-virgin olive oil in a medium non-stick skillet. Add 1 pound zucchini, sliced ¼ inch thick, and cook, stirring every 2 to 3 minutes, until tender and most of the slices are golden. Reduce heat; season with salt and freshly ground pepper to taste. Sprinkle with ¼ cup finely grated Parmesan cheese, cover and cook until the cheese is melted.

Per Serving: 83 calories; 5 g fat (1 g sat, 2 g mono); 5 mg cholesterol; 8 g carbohydrate; 5 g protein; 3 g fiber; 277 mg sodium; 594 mg potassium.

Orange-Infused Green Beans & Red Pepper

Preheat oven to 450°F. Toss ½ pound trimmed green beans and ½ thinly sliced red bell pepper with 1½ teaspoons extra-virgin olive oil, zest of ½ orange, ¼ teaspoon salt and ⅛ teaspoon crushed red pepper. Spread out on a rimmed baking sheet. Roast, turning once halfway through cooking, until tender and slightly wilted, about 10 minutes.

Per Serving: 78 calories; 4 g fat (1 g sat, 3 g mono); 0 mg cholesterol; 11 g carbohydrate; 2 g protein; 5 g fiber; 298 mg sodium; 318 mg potassium.

Roasted Corn with Basil-Shallot Vinaigrette

Preheat oven to 450°F. Toss 1½ cups fresh corn kernels with 1 tablespoon extra-virgin olive oil. Spread out on a rimmed baking sheet. Roast, stirring once, until some of the kernels begin to brown, about 15 minutes total. Stir together 2 tablespoons chopped fresh basil, 1½ teaspoons each minced shallot and red-wine vinegar, ¼ teaspoon salt and freshly ground pepper to taste in a small bowl. Add the corn to the bowl and toss to coat.

Per Serving: 165 calories; 8 g fat (1 g sat, 6 g mono); 0 mg cholesterol; 23 g carbohydrate; 4 g protein; 3 g fiber; 163 mg sodium; 332 mg potassium.

Roasted Corn with Basil-Shallot Vinaigrette

Sautéed Spinach with Toasted Sesame Oil

medium skillet over medium heat. Grate beets into the pan using the large-hole side of a box grater. Add 1 small minced garlic clove. Cook, stirring constantly, for 1 minute. Add 2 tablespoons water and bring to a simmer. Cover, reduce heat to low and cook until tender, about 8 minutes.

Steam: Cut beets into quarters. Place in a steamer basket over 1 inch of water in a large pot set over high heat. Cover and steam until tender, about 15 minutes.

4. Broccoli

Look for: Sturdy, dark-green spears with tight buds, no yellowing and a high floret-to-stem ratio.

Prep: Cut off florets; cut stalks in half lengthwise and then into 1-inch-thick half-moons.

Microwave: Place stems and florets in a medium glass baking dish. Cover tightly and microwave on High until tender, about 4 minutes.

Roast: Preheat oven to 500°F. Spread stems and florets on a baking sheet or in a pan large enough to hold them in a single layer. Coat with 1 1/2 teaspoons extra-virgin olive oil. Roast, turning once halfway through cooking, until tender and browned in places, about 10 minutes.

Steam: Place stems in a steamer basket over 1 inch of water (with 1 1/2 teaspoons lemon juice added to it) in a large pot set over high heat. Cover and steam for 2 minutes. Add florets; cover and continue steaming until tender, about 5 minutes more.

5. Brussels Sprouts

Look for: Tight, firm, small deep-green heads without yellowed leaves or insect holes. The sprouts should preferably still be on the stalk.

Prep: Remove from stalk, if necessary; peel off outer leaves; trim stem.

Braise: Place sprouts and 1/2 cup dry white wine in a medium skillet over medium-high heat. Cover and braise until tender, about 7 minutes. Remove sprouts with a slotted spoon; increase heat to high, add 1/2 teaspoon butter and reduce liquid to a glaze. Pour over sprouts.

Microwave: Place sprouts in a medium glass baking dish. Add 2 tablespoons broth (*or* water), cover tightly and microwave on High until tender, about 6 minutes.

Roast: Preheat oven to 500°F. Cut sprouts in half. Spread on a baking sheet or in a pan large enough to hold them in a single layer. Coat with 1 1/2 teaspoons extra-virgin olive oil. Roast, turning once halfway through cooking, until browned and tender, about 20 minutes.

Steam: Place sprouts in a steamer basket over 1 inch of water in a large pot set over high heat. Cover and steam until tender, 6 to 8 minutes.

6. Carrots

Look for: Orange, firm spears without any gray, white or desiccated residue on the skin. The greens should preferably still be attached.

Prep: Peel; cut off greens.

Microwave: Cut carrots into 1/8-inch-thick rounds. Place in a medium glass baking dish. Add 2 tablespoons broth (*or* white wine). Cover tightly and microwave on High until tender, about 3 minutes.

Roast: Preheat oven to 500°F. Cut carrots in half lengthwise then cut into 1 1/2-inch-long pieces. Spread on a baking sheet or in a pan large enough to hold them in a single layer. Coat with 1 teaspoon extra-virgin olive oil. Roast, turning once halfway through cooking, until beginning to brown, about 15 minutes.

Sauté: Cut carrots into 1/8-inch-thick rounds. Melt 1 1/2 teaspoons butter in a medium skillet over medium-low heat. Add carrots; stir and cook until tender, about 4 minutes. Add 1/2 teaspoon sugar; stir until glazed.

Steam: Cut carrots into 1/8-inch thick rounds. Place in a steamer basket over 1 inch of water in a large pot set over high heat. Cover and steam for 4 minutes.

7. Cauliflower

Look for: Tight white or purple heads without brown or yellow spots; the green leaves at the stem should still be attached firmly to the head, not limp or withered.

Prep: Cut into 1-inch-wide florets; discard core and thick stems.

Braise: Place florets in a medium skillet with ¼ cup dry white wine (*or* dry vermouth) and ¼ teaspoon caraway seeds. Bring to a simmer, reduce heat, cover and cook until tender, about 4 minutes.

Microwave: Place florets in a medium glass baking dish. Add 2 tablespoons dry white wine (*or* dry vermouth). Cover tightly and microwave on High until tender, about 4 minutes.

Roast: Preheat oven to 500°F. Spread florets on a baking sheet or in a pan large enough to hold them in a single layer. Coat with 1½ teaspoons extra-virgin olive oil. Roast, turning once halfway through cooking, until tender and beginning to brown, about 15 minutes.

Steam: Place florets in a steamer basket over 1 inch of water in a large pot set over high heat. Cover and steam for 5 minutes.

8. Corn

Look for: Pale to dark green husks with moist silks; each ear should feel heavy to the hand, the cob filling the husk well.

Prep: To remove kernels from the cob, stand an uncooked ear of corn on its stem end in a shallow bowl and slice the kernels off with a sharp, thin-bladed knife. This technique produces whole kernels that are good for adding to salads and salsas. If you want to use the corn kernels for soups, fritters or puddings, you can add another step to the process. After cutting the kernels off, reverse the knife and, using the dull side, press it down the length of the ear to push out the rest of the corn and its milk.

Grill: Husk corn and wrap the ears in foil. Preheat grill to high. Grill corn over direct heat, turning frequently, for 10 minutes. Carefully remove foil before serving.

Microwave: Husk corn and cut ears into thirds; place in a medium glass baking dish. Cover tightly and microwave on High until tender, about 4 minutes.

Sauté: Remove kernels from cobs. Melt 1 teaspoon butter in a medium skillet over medium heat. Add corn kernels; cook, stirring constantly, until tender, about 3 minutes.

Stir in ¼ teaspoon white-wine vinegar before serving.

Steam: Husk corn, then break or cut ears in half to fit in a steamer basket. Set over 1 inch of water in a large pot over high heat. Cover and steam until tender, about 4 minutes.

9. Eggplant

Look for: Smooth, glossy skins without wrinkles or spongy spots; each eggplant should feel heavy for its size.

Prep: Slice into ½-inch-thick rounds (peeling is optional).

Braise: Cut eggplant slices into cubes. Mix with ½ cup salsa. Pour into a pan and place over medium heat. Cover and cook, stirring often, until thick, about 15 minutes.

Grill: Preheat grill to medium-high; lightly oil rack. Brush eggplant slices lightly with extra-virgin olive oil. Grill over direct heat, turning once, until browned, about 8 minutes.

Roast: Preheat oven to 500°F. Brush both sides of eggplant slices with 1 teaspoon extra-virgin olive oil and arrange on a baking sheet or pan large enough to hold them in a single layer. Roast, turning once halfway through cooking, until tender, about 15 minutes.

Sauté: Cut eggplant slices into cubes; mix with 1 teaspoon salt. Let stand for 5 minutes, then blot dry with paper towels. Heat 1 teaspoon extra-virgin olive oil in a medium skillet over medium heat. Add the eggplant; cook until tender, stirring often, about 4 minutes.

10. Fennel

Look for: Compact, white, unbruised bulbs with brilliant green stalks and feathery fronds.

Prep: Cut off the stalks and fronds where they meet the bulb, remove any damaged outer layers, cut ¼ inch off the bottom and remove the core.

Braise: Cut bulb into 1-inch pieces. Heat 1½ teaspoons extra-virgin olive oil in a medium skillet over medium heat. Add fennel and 1 teaspoon dried rosemary, crushed. Cook 1 minute, stirring constantly. Add ¼ cup dry white wine (*or* dry vermouth). Cover, reduce heat and cook until tender, about 15 minutes.

Roast: Preheat oven to 500°F. Cut bulb into ¼-inch

pieces. Spread on a baking sheet or in a pan large enough to hold them in a single layer. Coat with I teaspoon extra-virgin olive oil. Roast, turning once halfway through cooking, until tender and beginning to brown, 18 to 20 minutes.

Steam: Cut bulb into I-inch pieces. Place in a steamer basket over I inch of water (with I teaspoon mustard seeds and I bay leaf added to it) in a large pot set over high heat. Cover and steam until tender, about 15 minutes.

II. Green Beans

Look for: Small, thin, firm beans.

Prep: Snip off stem ends.

Microwave: Place beans in a medium glass baking dish. Add 2 tablespoons broth (*or* water). Cover and microwave on High for 4 minutes.

Roast: Preheat oven to 500°F. Spread beans on a baking sheet or in a pan large enough to hold them in a single layer. Coat with I½ teaspoons extra-virgin olive oil. Roast, turning once halfway through cooking, until tender and beginning to brown, about 10 minutes.

Sauté: Heat I teaspoon walnut oil (*or* canola oil) in a medium skillet. Add beans; cook, stirring constantly, for 2 minutes.

Steam: Place beans in a steamer basket over I inch of water in a large pot set over high heat. Cover and steam for 5 minutes.

I2. Leeks

Look for: Long, thin stalks that do not bend and are not bruised; the outer layers should not be wrinkly or dried out.

Prep: Trim off the thick green leaves, leaving only the pale green and white parts; pull off damaged outer layers, leaving the root end intact. Split in half lengthwise. Under cold running water, fan out inner layers to rinse out grit and sand.

Braise: Place leeks in a large skillet with ¼ cup vegetable (*or* chicken broth), I sprig fresh rosemary (*or* 3 juniper berries and 3 black peppercorns). Bring to a simmer over high heat. Cover, reduce heat and cook until tender,

about 12 minutes. Serve warm or cold with a vinaigrette dressing, such as Maple-Mustard Vinaigrette (*page 226*).

Grill: Preheat grill to medium; lightly oil rack. Brush leeks with I½ teaspoons extra-virgin olive oil. Place over direct heat and grill, turning occasionally, until lightly browned, about 8 minutes.

Roast: Preheat oven to 500°F. Trim off root ends of leeks, slice in half crosswise and then into ¼-inch-thick slices lengthwise. Spread on a baking sheet or pan large enough to hold them in a single layer. Coat with I teaspoon extra-virgin olive oil. Roast, stirring once halfway through cooking, until browned and tender, 10 to 15 minutes.

Sauté: Thinly slice leeks into half-moons. Heat I½ teaspoons butter in a large skillet over medium heat. Add leeks; cook, stirring often, until softened and very aromatic, about 5 minutes.

I3. Onions

Look for: Firm onions with dry, papery skins. Avoid ones with green shoots or dark spots.

Prep: Trim stem end and remove papery skin.

Grill: Preheat grill; lightly oil rack. Cut through root end into quarters. Toss with extra-virgin olive oil and grill over direct heat, cut side down, until well-browned and tender, about 5 minutes per side. Season with salt and freshly ground pepper.

Roast: Cut through the root end into 8 wedges. Place in a pan large enough to hold them and toss with I½ teaspoons extra-virgin olive oil, 3 tablespoons balsamic vinegar and ¼ teaspoon salt. Cover with foil and bake until almost tender, about 45 minutes. Uncover and cook until soft and caramelized, 5 to 10 minutes more.

Sauté: Cut in half through the root end, remove the root and thinly slice vertically. Heat I tablespoon extra-virgin olive oil in a skillet over medium-high heat. Add onions and reduce heat to medium-low. Cook, stirring occasionally, until very tender and dark golden brown, about 45 minutes. Add a little water if necessary while cooking to prevent burning.

14. Peas

Look for: If fresh, look for firm, vibrant green pods without blotches and with the stem end still attached.

Prep: If fresh, zip open the hull, using the stem end as a tab, and release peas into a bowl. If frozen, do not defrost before using.

Microwave: Place peas in a glass baking dish; add 1 tablespoon water (*or* unsweetened apple juice). Cover tightly and microwave on High for 2 minutes.

Sauté: Heat 1 teaspoon butter in a medium skillet over medium heat. Add peas; cook, stirring often, until bright green, about 3 minutes.

Steam: Place peas in a steamer basket over 1 inch of water in a large pot set over high heat. Cover and steam for 2 minutes.

15. Potatoes, red-skinned or yellow-fleshed

Look for: Small potatoes with firm skins that are not loose, papery or bruised.

Prep: Scrub off any dirt (peeling is optional; the skin is fiber-rich and the nutrients are clustered about ½ inch below the skin).

Braise: Cut potatoes into ½-inch pieces. Place in a medium skillet with ¼ cup each broth and nonfat milk and ½ teaspoon butter. Bring to a simmer, cover, reduce heat and cook until tender and most of the liquid has been absorbed, about 20 minutes.

Roast: Preheat oven to 500°F. Halve potatoes then cut into ½-inch wedges. Spread on a baking sheet or in a pan large enough to hold them in a single layer. Coat with 1 teaspoon extra-virgin olive oil. Roast, stirring once halfway through cooking, until crispy and browned on the outside and tender on the inside, 20 to 25 minutes.

Sauté: Peel potatoes (if desired), then shred using the large-hole side of a box grater. Heat 1½ teaspoons canola oil in a medium nonstick skillet over medium heat. Add potatoes; reduce heat. Cook, pressing down with a wooden spoon, for 6 minutes. Flip the cake over and continue cooking until browned, about 5 minutes more.

Steam: Place potatoes in a steamer basket over 1 inch of water in a large pot set over high heat. Cover and steam until tender when pierced with a fork, about 10 minutes.

16. Spinach & Swiss Chard

Look for: Supple, deeply colored leaves without mushy spots.

Prep: Rinse thoroughly to remove sand; remove thick stems and shred leaves into 2-inch chunks. Rinse leaves again but do not dry.

Braise: Heat 1 teaspoon walnut oil (*or* canola oil) in a medium skillet over medium heat. Add spinach *or* chard; cook, stirring, until wilted. Add ¼ cup dry white wine (*or* dry vermouth). Cover, reduce heat, and cook for about 5 minutes. Uncover and cook until liquid is reduced to a glaze. Sprinkle 1 teaspoon balsamic vinegar (*or* rice vinegar) over the greens.

17. Squash, Delicata

Look for: Small, firm squash with bright yellow or orange skins that have green veins branching like lightning through them.

Prep: Cut squash in half lengthwise, scoop out the seeds and slice into thin half-moons (peeling is optional).

Microwave: Place squash slices in a medium glass baking dish with 2 tablespoons broth (*or* water). Cover tightly and microwave on High for 10 minutes.

Sauté: Melt 1 teaspoon butter in a medium skillet over medium heat. Add squash slices; cook, stirring frequently, until tender, about 10 minutes. Stir in a pinch of freshly grated nutmeg before serving.

Steam: Place squash slices in a steamer basket over 1 inch of water in a large pot set over high heat. Cover and cook until tender, about 6 minutes.

18. Squash, Summer & Zucchini

Look for: No breaks, gashes or soft spots; smaller squash (under 8 inches) are sweeter and have fewer seeds.

Prep: Cut off stem ends. Do not peel, but scrub off any dirt.

Grill: Preheat grill to medium; lightly oil rack. Cut squash lengthwise into ¼-inch slices. Brush squash slices lightly with 1½ teaspoons extra-virgin olive oil. Place over direct heat; grill, turning once, until marked and lightly browned, 3 to 4 minutes.

Roast: Preheat oven to 500°F. Cut squash lengthwise into ¼-inch-thick slices. Spread on a baking sheet or in a pan large enough to hold them in a single layer. Coat with 1 teaspoon extra-virgin olive oil. Roast, turning once halfway through cooking, until tender, about 10 minutes.

Sauté: Cut squash into ¼-inch-thick rings. Heat 1½ teaspoons extra-virgin olive oil in a medium skillet over medium heat. Add 1 small minced garlic clove and squash; cook, stirring frequently, until tender, about 7 minutes.

Steam: Cut squash into ½-inch-thick rings. Place in a steamer basket with ½ small onion, thinly sliced. Place over 1 inch of water in a large pot set over high heat. Cook until tender, about 5 minutes.

19. Sweet Potatoes

Look for: Taut, if papery, skins with tapered ends.
Prep: Scrub.
Braise: Peel sweet potatoes and cut into 1-inch pieces. Place in a medium skillet with ½ cup broth, ½ teaspoon honey and ¼ teaspoon dried thyme. Bring to a simmer over high heat; reduce heat, cover and cook until almost tender, about 15 minutes. Uncover, increase heat and cook until the liquid is reduced to a glaze, about 2 minutes.

Microwave: Place 1 to 2 medium sweet potatoes in a medium glass baking dish; pierce with a knife. Microwave on High until soft, 8 to 12 minutes. Let stand for 5 minutes.

Roast: Preheat oven to 500°F. Halve sweet potatoes, then cut into ½-inch wedges. Spread on a baking sheet or in a pan large enough to hold them in a single layer. Coat with 1 teaspoon extra-virgin olive oil. Roast, turning once halfway through cooking, until browned and tender, 20 to 25 minutes.

Steam: Peel sweet potatoes and cut into 1-inch pieces. Place in a steamer basket over 1 inch of water in a pot set over high heat. Cover and steam until tender, about 20 minutes.

20. Turnips

Look for: Smaller turnips with firm, white skins; they should feel heavy to the hand. The greens should preferably still be attached.

Prep: Cut off the root end and the greens; peel, then cut into thin slices.

Grill: Steam turnip slices (*see below*) for 5 minutes; meanwhile, preheat grill to medium-high and lightly oil rack. Place turnip slices over direct heat and grill, turning once, until lightly browned and tender, about 8 minutes.

Roast: Preheat oven to 500°F. Spread turnip slices on a baking sheet or in a pan large enough to hold them in a single layer. Coat with 1 teaspoon extra-virgin olive oil. Roast, turning once halfway through cooking, until tender, about 15 minutes.

Sauté: Cut turnip slices into matchsticks. Heat ½ teaspoon each butter and extra-virgin olive oil in a medium skillet over medium heat; add turnip matchsticks and cook, stirring frequently, until tender, about 12 minutes.

Steam: Place turnip slices in a steamer basket over 1 inch of water in a large pot set over high heat. Cover and cook until tender when pierced with a fork, about 12 minutes.

Grain-Cooking Guide

YIELD: ABOUT **1** CUP COOKED GRAIN.

	GRAIN	LIQUID (water/broth)	DIRECTIONS
BARLEY Quick-cooking	½ cup	I cup	Bring liquid to a boil; add barley. Reduce heat to low and simmer, covered, about 10 minutes.
Pearl	⅓ cup	I cup	Bring barley and liquid to a boil. Reduce heat to low and simmer, covered, about 30 minutes.
BULGUR	½ cup	¾ cup	Bring bulgur and liquid to a boil. Remove from the heat, cover and let stand until most of the liquid has been absorbed, 10-15 minutes.
COUSCOUS Whole-wheat	⅓ cup	⅞ cup	Bring liquid to a boil; stir in couscous. Remove from heat and let stand, covered, 5 minutes. Fluff with a fork.
QUINOA	⅓ cup	⅔ cup	Rinse in several changes of cold water. Bring quinoa and liquid to a boil. Reduce heat to low and simmer, covered, until tender and most of the liquid has been absorbed, 10-15 minutes. Fluff with a fork.
RICE Brown	⅓ cup	⅞ cup	Bring rice and liquid to a boil. Reduce heat to low and simmer, covered, until tender and most of the liquid has been absorbed, about 25 minutes. Let stand 5 minutes, then fluff with a fork.
Instant brown	⅔ cup	⅔ cup	Bring liquid to a boil. Stir in rice. Return to a boil. Reduce heat to low, cover and simmer for 5 minutes. Remove from the heat and stir, cover and let stand 5 minutes. Fluff with a fork.
Wild	½ cup	At least 4 cups	Cook rice in a large saucepan of lightly salted boiling water until tender, 40-50 minutes. Drain.
Instant wild	⅔ cup	⅔ cup	Bring liquid to a boil. Stir in rice. Return to a boil. Reduce heat to low, cover and simmer for 5 minutes. Drain.

Quick Desserts

EACH RECIPE MAKES **2** SERVINGS.

Baked Apples

Preheat oven to 350°F. Core 2 apples. Combine 4 teaspoons each chopped dried fruit and chopped toasted nuts, I teaspoon honey and a pinch of cinnamon; spoon into the apples. Place the apples in a small baking dish and pour ½ cup apple cider around them. Cover with foil. Bake until tender, about 45 minutes. Serve topped with plain yogurt.

Per Serving: 165 calories; 4 g fat (0 g sat, 2 g mono); 0 mg cholesterol; 35 g carbohydrate; 1 g protein; 4 g fiber; 2 mg sodium; 215 mg potassium.

Balsamic-Vinegar Spiked Strawberries

Hull and slice ½ pint strawberries. Place in a bowl and toss with I½ teaspoons sugar, or to taste. Sprinkle with I to I½ teaspoons balsamic (*or* red-wine vinegar). Let stand for 20 minutes before serving.

Per Serving: 37 calories; 0 g fat (0 g sat, 0 g mono); 0 mg cholesterol; 9 g carbohydrate; 0 g protein; 1 g fiber; 1 mg sodium; 112 mg potassium.

Bananas in Brown Sugar-Rum Sauce

Stir 2 tablespoons brown sugar, I teaspoon butter and ½ teaspoon canola oil in a medium skillet over medium heat until bubbling. Add 2 tablespoons dark rum, I teaspoon lime juice and ⅛ teaspoon ground cinnamon and cook until slightly thickened. Add 2 small, quartered bananas and cook, stirring, until tender. Divide between 2 bowls and top with a dollop of low-fat vanilla yogurt.

Per Serving: 208 calories; 4 g fat (2 g sat, 1 g mono); 6 mg cholesterol; 38 g carbohydrate; 2 g protein; 3 g fiber; 11 mg sodium; 399 mg potassium.

Chocolate Sauce

Sift together I½ tablespoons unsweetened cocoa powder and ¾ teaspoon each cornstarch and sugar in a small saucepan. Gradually whisk in I½ tablespoons skim milk. Whisk in 2 tablespoons corn syrup. Bring to a boil, whisking. Reduce heat to low and simmer until thickened. Remove from heat and whisk in ¼ teaspoon each canola oil and vanilla extract. Serve over scoops of vanilla frozen yogurt *or* raspberry sorbet.

Per Serving: 88 calories; 1 g fat (0 g sat, 1 g mono); 0 mg cholesterol; 21 g carbohydrate; 1 g protein; 1 g fiber; 20 mg sodium; 82 mg potassium.

Fresh Fruit with Lemon-Mint Cream

Whisk ¾ cup nonfat plain yogurt, ¼ cup each reduced-fat sour cream and sugar, 3 tablespoons lemon juice and I tablespoon finely chopped fresh mint until the sugar dissolves. Chill, covered, for I hour. Divide I cup fruit between 2 bowls (raspberries are especially delicious) and top with the lemon-mint cream.

Per Serving: 214 calories; 4 g fat (2 g sat, 1 g mono); 14 mg cholesterol; 43 g carbohydrate; 6 g protein; 4 g fiber; 65 mg sodium; 167 mg potassium.

Grilled Peach Sundaes

Preheat grill to high. Cut 2 peaches in half and remove the pits. Brush with canola oil. Grill until tender. Place 2 peach halves in each bowl and top with a scoop of nonfat vanilla frozen yogurt *or* fruit sorbet and toasted unsweetened coconut.

Per Serving: 154 calories; 4 g fat (2 g sat, 2 g mono); 0 mg cholesterol; 28 g carbohydrate; 4 g protein; 2 g fiber; 41 mg sodium; 319 mg potassium.

Marsala-Poached Figs over Ricotta

Place ½ cup quartered dried figs, ¼ cup Marsala (*or* port) and 2 teaspoons honey in a small saucepan. Bring to a boil, reduce heat and simmer until the figs soften and the wine is syrupy. Stir together ½ cup part-skim ricotta, 1 teaspoon sugar and ⅛ teaspoon vanilla extract. Divide between 2 bowls and top with the fig mixture and toasted slivered almonds.

Per Serving: 259 calories; 7 g fat (3 g sat, 3 g mono); 19 mg cholesterol; 45 g carbohydrate; 9 g protein; 5 g fiber; 86 mg sodium; 444 mg potassium.

Bananas in Brown Sugar-Rum Sauce

Old-Fashioned Fruit Crumble

Combine 1¼ cups fresh *or* frozen fruit with 1½ teaspoons each sugar, all-purpose flour and orange juice. Divide between two 6-ounce ovenproof ramekins. Combine ¼ cup old-fashioned oats, 3 tablespoons chopped almonds, 4 teaspoons brown sugar, 2½ teaspoons all-purpose flour and a pinch of cinnamon. Drizzle with 1 tablespoon canola oil and stir to combine. Sprinkle over the fruit mixture. Place on a baking sheet and bake at 400°F until fruit is bubbling and topping is golden, 20 to 25 minutes.

Per Serving: 265 calories; 13 g fat (1 g sat, 7 g mono); 0 mg cholesterol; 37 carbohydrate; 4 g protein; 4 g fiber; 1 mg sodium; 173 mg potassium.

Old-Fashioned Fruit Crumble

Pineapple-Coconut Frappe

Blend 1½ cups chopped pineapple, 1 cup low-fat milk, ⅓ cup "lite" coconut milk and 10 ice cubes in a blender until frothy.

Per Serving: 143 calories; 4 g fat (3 g sat, 1 g mono); 8 mg cholesterol; 23 g carbohydrate; 6 g protein; 2 g fiber; 78 mg sodium; 134 mg potassium.

Quick "Cheesecake"

Spread 4 whole-wheat graham crackers with 1 tablespoon part-skim ricotta cheese and 2 teaspoons jam.

Per Serving: 239 calories; 6 g fat (2 g sat, 1 g mono); 10 mg cholesterol; 42 g carbohydrate; 7 g protein; 2 g fiber; 259 mg sodium; 39 mg potassium.

Grilled Peach Sundaes

Quick "Cheesecake"

Raspberry-Mango Sundae

Strawberry Ice Cream Soda

Raspberry-Mango Sundae

Puree ½ cup thawed frozen raspberries, 1 tablespoon sugar and ¼ teaspoon lemon juice in a blender. Serve over scoops of nonfat vanilla frozen yogurt with diced mango and chopped toasted nuts.

Per Serving: 167 calories; 2 g fat (0 g sat, 2 g mono); 0 mg cholesterol; 35 g carbohydrate; 4 g protein; 2 g fiber; 41 mg sodium; 210 mg potassium.

Roasted Grapes

Preheat oven to 450°F. Separate ½ pound grapes into small clusters. Arrange the clusters in a single layer on a baking sheet. Drizzle with ¾ teaspoon extra-virgin olive oil and sprinkle with ⅛ teaspoon each kosher salt and freshly ground pepper to taste. Roast until the skins are slightly crisp but the grapes are still soft and juicy inside, about 15 minutes. Serve warm or at room temperature, with ¼ cup low-fat plain (or vanilla) yogurt for dipping.

Per Serving: 114 calories; 2 g fat (1 g sat, 1 g mono); 23 mg cholesterol; 23 g carbohydrate; 2 g protein; 1 g fiber; 171 mg sodium; 288 mg potassium.

Sautéed Pear Sundaes

Melt 1 teaspoon butter in a small nonstick pan. Add 1 sliced pear and cook, stirring occasionally, until golden and tender. Sprinkle with 2 teaspoons brown sugar, ⅛ teaspoon ground cinnamon and a pinch of ground ginger; stir until the sugar melts. Serve over scoops of nonfat frozen yogurt.

Per Serving: 160 calories; 2 g fat (1 g sat, 0 g mono); 5 mg cholesterol; 35 g carbohydrate; 3 g protein; 3 g fiber; 41 mg sodium; 220 mg potassium.

Seared Polenta with Chunky Blueberry Sauce

Combine ½ cup fresh or frozen blueberries, 2 tablespoons water, 1 tablespoon honey, ¼ teaspoon freshly grated lemon zest and 1½ teaspoons lemon juice in a small saucepan. Simmer until the sauce has thickened. Meanwhile, heat 1 teaspoon canola oil in a medium nonstick skillet. Cook 4 polenta slices until golden on both sides. Top with the blueberry sauce.

Per Serving: 145 calories; 2 g fat (0 g sat, 1 g mono); 0 mg cholesterol; 29 g carbohydrate; 2 g protein; 2 g fiber; 311 mg sodium; 39 mg potassium.

Strawberry Ice Cream Soda

Blend 1½ cups slightly softened nonfat vanilla frozen yogurt and 1⅓ cups hulled strawberries in a blender. Divide between 2 tall glasses and add 1 cup chilled club soda to each glass. Top each with ¼ cup nonfat vanilla frozen yogurt.

Per Serving: 191 calories; 0 g fat (0 g sat, 0 g mono); 1 mg cholesterol; 43 g carbohydrate; 7 g protein; 2 g fiber; 81 mg sodium; 387 mg potassium.

Stuffed Nectarines

Preheat oven to 350°F. Cut 1 nectarine in half and remove the pit. Place cut-side up in a small baking dish. Combine 4 crushed gingersnaps, 2 teaspoons melted butter, 1 teaspoon brown sugar and ½ teaspoon lemon juice; divide between the nectarine halves. Pour ½ cup orange juice around them. Cover with foil. Bake until tender, about 25 minutes. Serve with low-fat vanilla yogurt.

Per Serving: 176 calories; 5 g fat (3 g sat, 1 g mono); 11 mg cholesterol; 30 g carbohydrate; 2 g protein; 1 g fiber; 103 mg sodium; 361 mg potassium.

Toasted Pound Cake with Lemon Sauce

Combine 1½ tablespoons sugar, 1 teaspoon freshly grated lemon zest and ½ teaspoon cornstarch in a small saucepan. Gradually whisk in 1 tablespoon lemon juice and ¼ cup water. Bring to a boil, whisking constantly. Simmer until slightly thickened. Remove from the heat and whisk in ½ teaspoon butter. Serve over slices of toasted reduced-fat pound cake.

Per Serving: 210 calories; 2 g fat (1 g sat, 0 g mono); 3 mg cholesterol; 45 g carbohydrate; 3 g protein; 1 g fiber; 194 mg sodium; 74 mg potassium.

Tips & Notes

COOKING TIPS

To **blend hot liquids**: Hot liquids can splatter out of a blender when it's turned on. To avoid this, remove the center piece of the lid. Loosely cover the hole with a folded kitchen towel and turn the blender on. Better airflow will keep the contents from spewing all over the kitchen.

To **clean and debeard mussels**: Use a stiff brush to scrub as you rinse them under running water. Discard any mussels with broken shells or any whose shells remain open after you tap them lightly. Use a blunt knife to scrape off any barnacles and pull off the black fibrous "beard" as you wash them. Once you have debearded the mussels, cook them quickly because they don't live long afterwards.

To **crack whole spices**: Place them in a plastic bag and crush with the bottom of a heavy skillet or pulse in a spice or coffee grinder.

To **hard-boil eggs**: Place eggs in a single layer in a saucepan; cover with water. Bring to a simmer over medium-high heat. Reduce heat to low and cook at the barest simmer for 10 minutes. Remove from heat, pour out hot water and run a constant stream of cold water over the eggs until completely cooled.

To **heat tortillas**: Wrap tortillas in foil and bake at 300°F until steaming, about 10 minutes.

To **make croutons**: Toss 1 cup whole-grain bread cubes with 1 tablespoon extra-virgin olive oil and a pinch each of salt, pepper and garlic powder. Spread out on a baking sheet and toast at 350°F until crispy, turning occasionally, 15 to 20 minutes.

To **make fresh breadcrumbs**: Trim crusts from firm sandwich bread. Tear bread into pieces and process in a food processor until a coarse crumb forms. One slice of bread makes about ⅓ cup crumbs.

To **oil a grill rack**: Oil a folded paper towel, hold it with tongs and rub it over the rack. (Do not use cooking spray on a hot grill.)

To **peel and cut a mango**: 1. Slice both ends off the mango, revealing the long, slender seed inside. Set the fruit upright on a work surface and remove the skin with a sharp knife. 2. With the seed perpendicular to you, slice the fruit from both sides of the seed, yielding two large pieces. 3. Turn the seed parallel to you and slice the two smaller pieces of fruit from each side.

To debeard mussels.

To skin a salmon fillet.

To segment citrus.

To peel and cut a mango.

To **pit olives**: Press down on olives with the side of a heavy knife to split them open and make removing the pits easier.

To **poach chicken breasts**: Place boneless, skinless chicken breasts in a medium skillet or saucepan and add enough water to cover; bring to a boil. Cover, reduce heat to low and simmer gently until the chicken is cooked through and no longer pink in the middle, 10 to 12 minutes.

To **segment citrus**: With a sharp knife, remove the skin and white pith from the fruit. Working over a bowl, cut the segments from their surrounding membranes. Squeeze juice into the bowl before discarding membranes.

To **shave hard cheese**, such as Asiago, Parmesan or Pecorino Romano, use a vegetable peeler.

To **skin a salmon fillet**: Place it on a clean cutting board, skin-side down. Starting at one corner, slip the blade of a long knife between the fish flesh and the skin, holding the skin down firmly with your other hand. Gently push the blade along at a 30° angle, separating the fillet from the skin without cutting through either. Or have your fishmonger do it for you.

To **slice raw steak**: If you have a little extra time before dinner, put the steak in the freezer for about 20 minutes to help make it easier to slice thinly.

To **toast chopped nuts or seeds**: Cook in a small dry skillet over medium-low heat, stirring constantly, until fragrant and lightly browned, 2 to 4 minutes.

To **toast whole nuts**: Spread on a baking sheet and bake at 350°F, stirring occasionally, until fragrant and lightly browned, 7 to 9 minutes.

INGREDIENT NOTES

Capicola & pancetta: These are flavorful cured Italian meats. Capicola tends to be more spicy and pancetta more salty. They can be used to enhance flavors in Italian cooking. Find them in the deli section of the supermarket.

Chicken-flavored broth: For vegetarian recipes, chicken-flavored broth, a vegetarian broth that tastes like chicken, is a good option. Sometimes called "No-Chicken Broth," it can be found with other broths or natural foods at most supermarkets.

Chile-garlic sauce: A blend of ground chiles, garlic and vinegar, it's commonly used to add heat and flavor to Asian soups, sauces and stir-fries. It can be found in the Asian section of large supermarkets (sometimes labeled as chili-garlic sauce or paste) and keeps up to 1 year in the refrigerator.

Chipotle peppers: These are dried, smoked jalapeño peppers. They are often used to add heat and a smoky flavor to foods. Ground chipotle can be found in the specialty spice section of most supermarkets.

Chipotle peppers in adobo sauce: Canned smoked jalapeños, which add heat and smokiness to dishes; the adobo sauce alone adds a spicy zest without extra heat. Look for small cans with Mexican foods in large supermarkets. Once opened, chipotles will keep for up to 2 weeks in the refrigerator or 6 months in the freezer.

Chorizo: A spicy pork sausage seasoned with paprika and chili originally from Spain and often used in Mexican cooking. Chorizo can be made with raw or smoked pork. Some chorizo is sold precooked while others are raw. Remove raw chorizo from its casing and cook in a skillet over medium-high heat, crumbling with the back of a spoon, until cooked through before proceeding with your recipe. Chorizo is available at well-stocked supermarkets, specialty food stores or online at www.tienda.com, (800) 710-4304.

Coconut milk: Look for reduced-fat coconut milk (labeled "lite") in the Asian section of your market.

Crab meat in a pouch: Crab meat can be purchased in handy, 3.5-ounce, shelf-stable pouches—usually in the same section as canned tuna.

Cream sherry: A fortified wine that is slightly sweeter than dry sherry. An opened bottle can be stored in a cool, dry place for months—unlike wine, which starts to decline within hours of being uncorked.

Duck breast: Boneless duck breast halves range widely in weight, from about ½ to 1 pound, depending on the breed of duck. They can be found in most supermarkets in the poultry or specialty-meat sections or online at www.mapleleaffarms.com, (800) 348-2812 or www.dartagnan.com, (800) 327-8246.

Fish sauce: A pungent Southeast Asian sauce made from salted, fermented fish. Found in the Asian section of large supermarkets and in Asian specialty markets.

Five-spice powder: Often a blend of cinnamon, cloves, fennel seed, star anise and Szechuan peppercorns, five-spice powder was originally considered a cure-all miracle blend encompassing the five elements (sour, bitter, sweet, pungent, salty). Look for it in the super-market spice section.

French green lentils: Smaller and firmer than brown lentils, they cook more quickly, in about 20 minutes. They can be found in natural-foods stores and some larger supermarkets.

Goat cheese: Also know as chèvre (French for goat), goat cheese is earthy-tasting and slightly tart. Fresh goat cheese is creamy and commonly available. Aged goat cheese has a nutty, sharp flavor and is drier and firmer. Look for aged goat cheese in a well-stocked cheese section at larger supermarkets and specialty cheese shops.

Herbes de Provence: A mixture of dried herbs commonly used in the south of France. You can find commercial mixtures in the supermarket spice section and at specialty stores, but it is easy to make your own. Mix 1 tablespoon each (or equal proportions) dried thyme, rosemary, oregano, marjoram and savory in a small jar. If desired, add a pinch each of dried lavender and crushed aniseed.

Hoisin sauce: This dark brown, thick, spicy-sweet sauce is made with soybeans and a complex mix of spices. Look for it in the Chinese section of supermarkets and in Asian markets.

Hominy: White or yellow corn that has been treated with lime to remove the tough hull and germ. Dried, ground hominy is the main ingredient in grits. Canned, cooked hominy can be found near the beans in the Mexican section of large supermarkets.

Korean chili powder (*gochu galu*)**:** This powder is made from thin red peppers that are sun-dried on woven mats or strung together and hung from the eaves of thatch-roofed houses throughout the countryside. Find it in Korean or Asian markets and store, airtight, in the refrigerator or freezer.

Manchego: A nutty-flavored sheep's milk cheese from Spain. Find it in well-stocked supermarkets or specialty cheese stores.

Marsala: A fortified wine that is a flavorful and economical addition to many sauces. An opened bottle can be stored in a cool, dry place for months—unlike wine, which declines within hours of being uncorked.

Mirin: A low-alcohol rice wine essential to Japanese cooking. Look for it in the Asian or gourmet-ingredients section of your supermarket. An equal portion of sherry or white wine with a pinch of sugar may be substituted for mirin.

Miso: Fermented bean paste made from barley, rice or soybeans used in Japanese cooking to add flavor to soups, sauces, salad dressings. A little goes a long way because of its concentrated, salty taste. Miso is available in different colors, depending on the type of grain or bean and how long it's been fermented. In general, the lighter the color, the more mild the flavor. Find in the refrigerated section with soy products. It will keep, in the refrigerator, for more than a year.

Oyster sauce: A richly flavored condiment made from oysters and brine often used in Asian cooking. Vegetarian oyster sauces substitute mushrooms for the oysters. Both can be found in the Asian section of large supermarkets, at Asian specialty markets or online at www.asianfoodgrocer.com, (888) 482-2742.

Pancetta. *See* **Capicola & pancetta**

Precooked diced potatoes: Look for these in the refrigerated section of most supermarket produce departments, near other fresh, prepared vegetables.

Quinoa: This delicately flavored grain was a staple in the ancient Incas' diet. It is available in most natural-foods stores and the natural-foods sections of many supermarkets. Toasting the grain before cooking enhances its flavor, and rinsing removes any residue of saponin, quinoa's natural, bitter protective covering.

Red curry paste: A blend of chile peppers, garlic, lemongrass and galanga (a root with a flavor similar to ginger). Look for it in jars or cans in the Asian section of the supermarket or specialty stores. Refrigerate for up to 6 months.

Rice flour: Made from finely milled white rice, it is often used in Asian cooking for desserts and to thicken sauces. Look for it in Asian markets or the natural-foods section of your supermarket.

Scallops: Be sure to request "dry" scallops, which have not been treated with sodium tripolyphosphate (STP). They are more flavorful and will brown the best.

Shao Hsing: Also known as *Shaoxing*, this is a seasoned rice wine available in most Asian specialty markets and some larger supermarkets' Asian sections.

Sherry (*see also* **cream sherry**)**:** The "cooking sherry" sold in many supermarkets can be surprisingly high in sodium. We prefer dry sherry, sold with other fortified wines in your wine or liquor store.

Sole: The term "sole" is widely used for many types of flatfish from both the Atlantic and Pacific. Flounder and Atlantic halibut are included in the group that is often identified as sole or grey sole. The best choices are Pacific, Dover, Petrale or English sole. Other sole and flounder are overfished.

Sriracha: Named after a port city in Thailand, this is a spicy sauce made from hot chiles, garlic, vinegar and sugar. It comes in a plastic squeeze bottle and can be found in large supermarkets or Asian specialty stores.

Stir-fry vegetables: Frozen bagged mixes of cut vegetables are appropriate for a stir fry. We prefer Seapoint Farms brand stir-fry mixes because they include the best variety of vegetables (often including shelled edamame) and they taste delicious. They are available in large supermarkets and natural foods stores.

Tofu: "Soybean curd" is made by heating soymilk and a curdling agent in a process similar to dairy cheesemaking. Allowed to stand and thicken, the curds form silken tofu. When stirred and separated from the whey, the pressed curds, with their spongier texture, are known as "regular" tofu. The longer the pressing, the firmer and denser the tofu—soft, firm or extra-firm.

TIPS FOR TWO

As hard as we tried not to have "leftovers" of things, it was just bound to happen. So we've created Tips for Two with storage tips and ideas on how to use leftovers.

Apricot nectar: Storage: Refrigerate leftover nectar for up to 1 week. Uses: Add to smoothies; whisk into salad dressing; combine with sparkling water for a refreshing non-alcoholic beverage.

Avocado: Storage: Although browning is inevitable, less browning is possible if you keep the pit in the half you're storing and wrap it tightly in plastic wrap; scrape off the discolored part, if desired, before using. Uses: Mash with reduced-fat mayonnaise and use as a sandwich spread; dice and sprinkle on top of scrambled eggs; toss in salad.

Beans, canned: Storage: Refrigerate for up to 3 days. Uses: Add to green salads and soups; mash with garlic powder and chopped fresh herbs for a quick dip; make Spiced Pinto Beans (*page 232*).

Broth: Storage: Leftover canned broth keeps up to 5 days in the refrigerator or up to 3 months in your freezer. Leftover broths in aseptic packages keep for up to 1 week in the refrigerator. Uses: Add to soups, sauces, stews; use for cooking rice and grains; add a little when reheating leftovers to prevent them from drying out.

Cabbage: Storage: Refrigerate for up to 1 week. Uses: Add to salads or soup; make Vinegary Coleslaw (*page 227*) or Warm Apple-Cabbage Slaw (*page 228*).

Coconut milk: Storage: Refrigerate for up to 4 days or freeze for up to 2 months. Uses: Make Coconut-Lime Dressing (*page 29*; keeps up to 3 days in the refrigerator*); drizzle on sliced fresh fruit for a quick dessert; use instead of water or broth when cooking rice; make Pineapple-Coconut Frappe (*page 241*).

Herbs, fresh: Storage: Wrap the root end in damp paper towels and store in a sealed plastic bag for up to 5 days or place the root end in a glass of water, loosely cover with a plastic bag, and store in the refrigerator for up to 1 week. Uses: Chop and add to salads, sauces, grains, soups, salad dressings and omelets; stir into softened butter to slather on corn on the cob or dab on grilled steak.

Italian turkey sausage links: Storage: Store in the refrigerator for up to 1 day; wrap in foil, seal in plastic and freeze up to 3 months. Uses: Sauté with peppers and onions and serve on a bun or with brown rice; boil, slice and add to omelets, soups or use on pizza.

Kale: Storage: Refrigerate, preferably in a perforated plastic bag, for 5 to 10 days. Uses: Substitute kale for chard in Sautéed Swiss Chard with Chile & Garlic (*page 232*); chop and add during the last 4 minutes while cooking pasta; sauté thinly sliced kale and minced garlic in extra-virgin olive oil and use for an omelet filling or stir into scrambled eggs.

Mango chutney: Storage: Refrigerate for up to 6 months. Uses: Whisk with yogurt for a quick dressing, dip or marinade; serve alongside grilled meat, fish or chicken; blend with reduced-fat cream cheese for a zingy spread.

Marinara sauce: Storage: Refrigerate for up to 1 week or freeze for up to 3 months. Uses: Spread on toasted whole-wheat English muffin halves and top with cheese for a quick snack; use for making lasagna; toss with roasted eggplant or other roasted vegetables.

Olives: Shopping: Buy just what you need at an olive bar or salad bar. Storage: Refrigerate for up to 6 months. Uses: Sprinkle on salads; toss with chopped fresh herbs and a little extra-virgin olive oil for a quick appetizer; pit, chop and add to your favorite pasta sauce.

Pork tenderloin: Storage: Tightly wrap and freeze any unused portion for up to 6 months. Uses: Dice and add to soups; add strips to stir-fries; sauté with potatoes and onions for a quick hash.

Tofu: Storage: Rinse leftover tofu, place in a storage container and cover with water; it keeps up to 4 days in the refrigerator if the water is changed every day or 2; freeze tofu for up to 5 months. (Freezing tofu yields a pleasingly chewy result that some people prefer. Don't be surprised if the frozen tofu turns a light shade of caramel.) Uses: Crumble and use instead of the meat in your favorite tuna or chicken salad recipe; dice and add to a vegetable stir-fry; add leftover silken tofu to smoothies.

Tomatoes, diced, canned: Storage: Refrigerate up to 1 week or freeze for up to 3 months. Uses: Add to soups and salsa; use to bulk up marinara sauce; add to an omelet with sliced green onions and shredded pepper Jack cheese.

Tomato paste: Storage: Refrigerate for up to 1 week or freeze for up to 3 months. Uses: Add to soups, chilis and sauces; stir into rice with oregano and cilantro to serve alongside Mexican dishes.

Water chestnuts: Storage: Store in the refrigerator, covered with water; they keep for up to 1 month if water is changed daily. Uses: Add to a stir-fry; toss in a green salad; add some crunch to a favorite chicken or tuna salad; make Asian Brown Rice (*page 228*).

Special Indexes

HEALTHY WEIGHT

ENTREES WITH THE **Healthy**){ **Weight** ICON: CALORIES ≤ 350, CARBS ≤ 33g, TOTAL FAT ≤ 20g, SAT FAT ≤ 10g

(*For more information on our nutrition guidelines, see page 4.*)

ENTREES READY TO EAT IN **30** MINUTES OR LESS:

TOTAL TIME: 15-20 MINUTES

Chicken & Turkey
Curried Squash & Chicken Soup, 56
Grilled Chicken with Chipotle-Orange
    Glaze, 127
Marmalade Chicken, 117
Turkey & Fontina Melts, 151

Fish & Seafood
Crab Salad-Stuffed Pitas, 181
Pacific Sole with Oranges & Pecans,
    176
Poached Salmon with Creamy Piccata
    Sauce, 159
Smoked Trout Hash with Mustard
    Greens, 170
Tuna & Red Pepper Antipasto, 37
Tuna-Potato Croquettes, 168

Beef & Pork
Chili-Rubbed Steaks & Pan Salsa, 192
Cider Vinegar-&-Molasses-Glazed Pork
    Chops, 207
Migas with Chorizo, 217
Pork & Red Pepper Hash, 213
Pork Cutlets with Cumberland Sauce,
    206

Vegetarian
Black Bean-Smothered Sweet Potatoes,
    100
Spinach & Dill Frittata, 104

TOTAL TIME: 25-30 MINUTES

Chicken, Duck & Turkey
Caesar Salad Three Ways, 34
Captiva Shrimp & Chicken Salad, 33
Chicken Fajita Wraps, 121
Chicken Parmesan Sub, 131
Creamy Artichoke & Spinach Soup, 64
Fusilli with Italian Sausage & Arugula,
    148
Jimmo's Chicken & Okra, 113
Madras Chicken & Broccoli Salad, 32
Miso Chicken Stir-Fry, 135
New Mexican Posole, 55
Rustic Mexican Stew, 54
Spinach & Beet Salad with Chicken, 26
Stewed Chicken Thighs with Dried
    Fruits, 112
Stir-Fried Chile-Garlic Duck, 136
Sweet & Savory Cutlets, 150
Tarragon Chicken, 122
Tea Trade Chicken, 125
Tex-Mex Taco Salad, 43
Turkey Cutlets with Lemon-Caper
    Sauce, 145
Turkey Marsala, 144
Turkey Scallopini with Apricot Sauce,
    141
White Chili, 62

Fish & Seafood
Beer-Battered Fish Tacos with Tomato &
    Avocado Salsa, 169
Blackened Salmon Po' Boy, 165
Broiled Salmon with Miso Glaze, 158
Captiva Shrimp & Chicken Salad, 33
Caesar Salad Three Ways, 34
Marinated Mussel Salad, 40
Salsa-Roasted Salmon, 161
Salt & Pepper Shrimp, 179
Southeast Asian Scallops & Greens, 41
Spicy Cioppino, 67
Spring Salad with Tarragon Vinaigrette,
    39

Beef, Pork & Lamb
Asian Salisbury Steaks, 201
Coffee Bean & Peppercorn Steak, 190
Cube Steak Milanese, 202
Grilled Rib-eye Steak with Tomato
    Salad & Chimichurri, 188
Grilled Steak with Beets & Radicchio,
    195
Herb-Coated Filet Mignon, 193
Korean Beef Stir-Fry, 196
Lamb & Eggplant Ragu, 222
Marrakech Grilled Steak & Sweet
    Potatoes, 191
Orzo with Lamb, Olives & Feta, 220
Penne with Vodka Sauce & Capicola,
    214
Pork Chops with Maple-Mustard Sauce,
    203
Pork Loin Chops with Mushrooms &
    Thyme, 204
Pork Tenderloin with Gingered Mango
    Sauce, 212
Pork with Dried Apples & Prosciutto,
    208
Quick French Onion Soup, 68
Spicy Potato & Kale Soup, 71
Tex-Mex Taco Salad, 43

Vegetarian
Caramelized Onion & Green Olive
    Pizzas, 97
Citrus-Scented Black Bean Soup with
    Chipotle Cream, 78
Corn & Tomato Pizzas, 96
Crispy Seitan Stir-Fry, 108
Greek Salad with Tofu, 48
Grilled Vegetable & Feta Panini, 95
Indian-Spiced Kale & Chickpeas, 101
Miso Vegetable Soup, 77
No-Bake Macaroni & Cheese, 88
Orecchiette with Broccoli Rabe &
    Chickpeas, 84
Orzo Salad with Chickpeas & Artichoke
    Hearts, 49
Pomodoro Pasta with White Beans &
    Olives, 92
Sweet Potato & Black Bean Chili, 79
Tofu Cutlets with Green Olives &
    Prunes, 103
Tunisian Vegetable Tagine, 75

Comprehensive Recipe Index

Page numbers in italics indicate photographs.

CONTRIBUTORS

Our thanks to the fine cooks whose work has appeared in EATINGWELL *Magazine.*

Farrell-Kingsley, Kathy: Roasted Grapes, 242
Hae-Jin Lee, Cecilia: Spicy Chicken Soup (*Dak Yookgaejang*), 61
Herr, Susan: Black Bean-Smothered Sweet Potatoes, 100
Riccardi, Victoria Abbott: Warm Arugula Salad with Chicken & Chèvre, 24
Simmons, Marie: Pomodoro Pasta with White Beans & Olives, 92
Weinstein, Bruce & Mark Scarbrough: Salsa-Roasted Salmon, 161; Pacific Sole with Oranges & Pecans, 176; Barbecued Mussels, 183; Saffron-Scented Mussels, 184; Pork Loin Chops with Mushrooms & Thyme, 204